MY HEART IS AN AUTUMN GARAGE

ANNE THÉRIAULT

Thought Catalog Books
Brooklyn, NY

THOUGHT CATALOG BOOKS

Copyright © 2015 by The Thought & Expression Co.

All rights reserved. Published by Thought Catalog Books, a division of The Thought & Expression Co., Williamsburg, Brooklyn.

For general information and submissions: manuscripts@thoughtcatalog.com.

First edition, 2015
ISBN 978-1517753832
10 9 8 7 6 5 4 3 2 1

Founded in 2010, Thought Catalog is a website and imprint dedicated to your ideas and stories. We publish fiction and non-fiction from emerging and established writers across all genres.

Cover photography by © Audrey Reid

AUTHOR'S NOTE

All names have been changed.

1.

Imagine that sadness is a real, physical place, a country, even, a name that you might find stamped on a passport.

Take a moment to create an image of that land in your head – the vast grey-green fields, the shadowy hills in the distance, the sky always threatening rain. Bordering the fields are dank, dripping forests filled with the rank stink of malignant vegetation undercut by the wistfully sweet smell of decomposition and decay. Dread hangs heavy in the air, like a fog that never lifts.

Picture the people, now – the plodding, round-shouldered denizens, their heads bowed from years of grinding misery. This is the native population. There are visitors, too, tourists, you might call them; some only stay for a handful of days or a few weeks, while others wind up living there for years at a time. If you're lucky, you might be one of the handful of people who only make the journey to Sadness once or twice in a lifetime; if you're like me, you'll find yourself there much more frequently. If you're there often enough, you might even consider buying property – the cost of living is low, and the only fees and taxes necessary are your happiness and well-being, a price that you've already paid on the journey there.

I like to think that I keep a sort of vacation home there.

Like, Oh, you winter in Florida? How nice.

I, myself, winter in Sadness.

Travelling to Sadness is easy; you don't need a visa or a passport. You don't even need a car. The border agents are gentle, deceptively kind – they don't ask too many questions, don't require any kind of documentation. They don't even need to know how long you'll be staying, mostly because they don't really care if you ever leave. Sadness has a very lax immigration policy.

I like to picture my house in Sadness sometimes, imagining what this metaphorical beauty might look like. It would be on the edge of a weed-choked lake, I think, a sort of gloomy cesspool full of slippery water plants and enormous leeches. The house itself would be a rickety old wooden affair, paint peeling and porch lurching dangerously to one side. The front yard would be overgrown, the grass knee-high and speckled with wildflowers. The path through the yard would be paved with flagstones worn smooth by years and years of comings and goings; the steps leading up to the front door would groan a long complaint under even the slightest weight. The first word that would come to mind when looking at the house would be *decrepit*.

Still, though, people would say that I did the best that I could with what I had.

Inside, for instance, it would smell warmly of spices and polished wood, with just the faintest whiff of saltwater and musty damp. All of my favourite regrets would be kept out on display, carefully arranged in chronological order, so that I could easily revisit them whenever I wanted. Old family photographs would line the walls, my Kodachrome self front and centre, her peaked little face wanting to know why I've let her down. There would be shrines erected to all most difficult times in my life – for example, the first two months of my son's life, which passed in a suicidal haze of postpartum depression – at which I could kneel and bow my head in deep devotion whenever the need struck me. Everything else, all of the little thoughts that caused me to feel shame or guilt or anxiety, would neatly filed away in the miniature Dewey Decimal drawers of an old library cabinet.

My house would be filled with these things – things like library cabinets and rotary dial telephones and bright plastic cassette tapes – that have no place in the modern world. Sometimes I would find them washed up on the edge of my little lake, like so much nostalgic flotsam and jetsam; other times I might manage to drag them with me, back from the real world, in an effort to save them from their slow decline into obsolescence. I would love these things desperately, even though their presence would fill me with a dirty-sweet sadness, trapping me forever in the memory of a past that I can never fully recreate. I would cling to these things, even though I would know that that clinging is only making my life harder to live.

People think that it's hard to love when you're sad, but the truth is that it's painfully easy. It's so easy to love too much, too hard, too fast, and this reckless loving is what undoes you in the end. Over and over again you crack your chest open to show off your bloody, still-beating heart, daring someone, anyone, to slide a hand in and touch it. And they do. They do.

And even though it hurts, you love them for it.

It's your love that pushes you right over the edge.

I love Sadness, too, even though it makes my heart ache and ache. It's comfortingly familiar, one of the biggest constants in my life so far. I've certainly lived here longer than I have anywhere else over the course of my somewhat peripatetic life. Sadness, more than anywhere else, is my home.

2.

How did I even get here in the first place?

I've often wondered this, both for my own sake and because others want to know the answer, too. It's the question that goes politely unasked whenever I tell people about my struggles with mental health, but I know that it's there, on the tips of their tongues, as they take a moment to step back and re-evaluate me. There's always that pause during which other people consider how this information, this invisible malignity, will affect their internal image of me. There's always that brief space of time in which they have to recalibrate what they know about me, mentally disassembling everything that they've been certain of so far and then figuring out how the pieces will fit back together now that this new information has been added. A time in which they quickly wonder, illogically and to their embarrassment, about the possibility of contagion.

I know what they're thinking:

She looks so normal. If she's crazy, then I'm crazy. And I'm not crazy.

How could she be crazy? How did this happen to her?

More importantly, how can I stop this from happening to me?

I can't really answer any of these questions, especially not the last one. All that I can do is lay out the map of my life and try to interpret what all the complicated twists and turns might mean. If they mean anything at all.

3.

If I were the type to self-mythologize, then I might start with my birthday: August 6th, 1982. If I were the type to think that there are no coincidences in this life, then I might point out that I was born at 3:37 in the morning on the 37th anniversary of the atomic bombing of Hiroshima. I might mention that three and seven are my lucky numbers, that thirty seven is both the first irregular prime and the number of plays that Shakespeare is thought to have written (counting Henry IV as three parts), and that NGC 37 is a spiral galaxy in the constellation Phoenix. I might tell you that these numbers were significant in some way, though if pressed for details I wouldn't be able to explain *why* what was.

If I were the type of person who believed in signs and omens, I might say that it makes perfect sense for a person born on the anniversary of such devastation should come into this world hardwired for sadness. It makes perfect sense for a historical event that turned people into shadows –

literal shadows – to leave me with a few shadows of my own. It makes perfect sense that, being born in the metaphorical wake of one of the most frightening moments of the 20th century, I might find myself to be just a little bit metaphorically haunted.

I mean, if I were that type.

If I were someone who accepted the idea of genetic memory, who believed that thought and feeling and physical sensation could be coded into our DNA, I might mention my Acadian ancestors. I might tell you all about the Grand Dérangement of 1755, the carefully orchestrated deportation of the Acadian population of Nova Scotia. I might tell you about how my forebears were herded onto boats like cattle to be shipped off to places like Boston or Maine or specially-built internment camps in England. I might tell you that less than half of the Acadian population survived this expulsion.

If I thought that concepts like culture and homeland were necessary for creating a sense of security and personal identity, then I might point out that I grew up without either. I might mention that, like many of my Acadian contemporaries, I grew up deep in the diaspora, several generations removed from the language and traditions and the raw, physical landscapes that shaped my ancestors' way of life. I might tell you that I've never felt any real sense of belonging to one place or another; no matter where I go, I always feel transient and rootless. I might say that I'm not exactly certain what other people feel when they talk about *home*, but I suspect that their thoughts and associations with that word differ greatly from my own. I might even go so far as to say that I've never had a home, not really – just a series of buildings that I've lived in.

I might say that sadness and emptiness and not-belonging were as assured at the moment of my conception as the fact that I have brown eyes, a cleft chin and impossibly tiny feet.

I mean, I might.

Then again, I might not. Maybe my depression is just a biological fact, a wayward misfiring of neurons. Maybe my moods can be explained by soundly scientific reasons that defy mythologizing or romanticizing. Maybe my chronic sadness is nothing more than my particular prize in the genetic lottery.

But that's not a very satisfying answer, is it?

4.

I used to think that my first forays into depression happened in my early teens, the result of a bad combination of hormones, loneliness and poor coping skills. But now that I'm taking a long, hard look back at my life, I have to wonder if all of this began much, much earlier.

I've always been quick to cry, and I have a remarkable ability to burst into tears over just about anything. Sometimes, if I'm feeling particularly anxious and rotten, I'll make myself cry on purpose, because I know that the release of tension will make me feel better. At school the other kids called me *crybaby*, a term that I still sometimes use to describe myself. I've come to accept the fact that some people deal with their feelings by talking, shouting, or banging things around, whereas other people cope by scrunching up their faces and leaking saltwater from their eyes; I just happen to be in the latter camp. But does the tendency to cry easily necessarily indicate a propensity for depression?

Maybe not, but when you combine it with my distinct talent for reflection and self-criticism, it might begin to offer a few clues.

Let's start out with the fact that I've always known that I was *bad*. I can't quite explain how or why, although I'll try, but I just plain knew that I wasn't a good girl. I wasn't a good girl and, in the perceptively nuanced logic of childhood, the absence of good could only mean bad. I felt that all of my natural tendencies and inclinations made me want to do exactly the opposite of whatever I was supposed to be doing, and it was only by carefully monitoring my desires and curbing my bad thoughts that I could manage to pass myself off as a decent person. The funny thing was that the vast majority of the time I was able to follow the rules and do what was expected of me, but that didn't make me cut myself any slack. It was as if my actions weren't what determined my character so much as that awful *wanting*. As if even just thinking about misbehaving was as bad as the misbehaving itself.

I remember once, in kindergarten, our teacher told us that those of us who thought that we'd been well-behaved that week could spend the last hour of the school day painting pictures as a special treat. Figuring that my teacher could see into my heart and knew what a rotten little girl I was, I quietly went over to the reading corner and took out a book. Although I couldn't think of anything specific that I'd done that week that would or could bar me from painting, I knew that I, as a person, was not deserving of any kind of reward for my behaviour.

At one point I looked up from my book and caught the teacher looking at me. My eyes caught hers and we stared at each other for a moment before she turned around to help someone with their smock. I knew that her silence meant that I'd made the right choice.

In the first grade, I started acting out more, partly because of my sister's birth and partly because of my babysitter's son. This boy, who was the same age as me, kept in a sort of fearful thrall. He did whatever he wanted – broke into his neighbour's garage and poured oil and windshield wiper fluid all over the floor, pulled down his pants and peed on the slide at the park, dragged me into their basement and exposed himself to me, threatening to say that I'd kicked him if I refused to touch *it* – and when I tried to tell on him, my babysitter somehow twisted it around and put the blame on me. Eventually I stopped saying anything, figuring that I would just have to grin and bear it. (Years later, in a fit of guilt over having touched a boy's penis, I would confess everything to my mother. Her response – *oh Annie, why didn't you tell me?* – only made me feel guiltier.)

My "acting out" was fairly tame – coming in late from recess, smudging another girl's artwork, sticking my hands down my pants in a way that seemed to both gross out and entertain the other kids – but I still won myself several trips to the principal's office. Whenever this happened, I felt equal parts shame and vindication; now, at last, everyone was seeing how truly awful I was.

I don't want to make it sound like I was entirely down on myself as a kid; in fact, in many ways the opposite was true. I knew that I was one of the smartest kids in my class, for example, and I knew that I was pretty, all golden-blond hair and almond-shaped eyes. I even sometimes knew how to use those things to my advantage. But I also knew that being smart and pretty weren't worth anything next to whether my parents or teachers or God or Jesus thought that I was a good.

5.

When I was ten I drew a picture of my four best friends with myself conspicuously absent. Underneath the picture, I wrote:

ANNE IS DEAD.

I don't recall why I drew that picture – probably some stupid fight or other – but I do remember how powerful it made me feel. I thought about how sad they would feel if I died. And I thought, I could kill myself, and I would be responsible for that sadness.

The idea that I could somehow elicit that kind of emotion from someone else was strangely intoxicating.

One of my friends must have turned that picture over to the teacher, because a few days later I was called to the principal's office. She wanted to talk to me about what I'd written, of course. I was deeply embarrassed, and told her that it had all been a bad joke. She kept pressing me to admit that something was wrong, all but begging me to confess that the picture was part of something bigger, but I was adamant. Eventually she gave up and sent me back to class.

As I was leaving her office, though, I caught her looking at me askance, and I knew that we were both wondering the same thing:

Had I really meant what I'd written?

Maybe.

Probably not.

But still. Maybe.

6.

When I was eleven, I bought a bright orange notebook and glued picture of a porcupine to the front cover. In this book, which I referred to as my *journal*, I wrote about how much I hated my life; I hated my school, hated my family, hated the way I looked. I wrote about how worried I was that my friends didn't like me. I wrote about how everything I did seemed wrong; even at that age I felt like I couldn't get my shit together.

Most of all, I wrote over and over, in embarrassingly florid prose, about how I wished that I could die. I didn't really know what I meant by that, but I wrote it all the same. Those words carried an intoxicating autonomy and power and, even if I wasn't sure how or why it felt good to write them, I knew that they made me feel important. Special.

I wasn't depressed; not yet, anyway. But I was trying sadness on like a tatty old sequined dress – does this fit me? Does this look right? Does this suit my personality?

7.

At the age of thirteen my life fell apart. My parents separated. My father closed his law firm, declared bankruptcy and moved to Toronto to live with my aunt. My mother, sisters and I moved into low-income housing; our family went on welfare to help supplement my mother's income as a college secretary. My youngest sister, who was two, hated her new babysitter, and would scream whenever I dropped her off in the morning and cling to me for hours when I picked her up at night. She wouldn't even let the babysitter change her diaper, so when I took her home I had to deal with a stinking mess that she'd been sitting in for hours and hours. Suddenly my life was a far cry from what it had been even a few weeks before.

Most of my afternoons and evenings were devoted to babysitting my sisters while my mother worked late and took night classes. It wasn't as if I had anything better to do with my time, though; in the midst of all this upheaval at home I'd suddenly become incredibly unpopular at school. In the span of a few months I went from being a pretty adorable little kid to a wretched-looking teenager with terrible acne. I didn't know how to dress my changing body, and in any case didn't have the money to buy new clothes, so I wore baggy sweats and hand-me-downs from my aunt. That same year, my four best friends decided collectively that they didn't want to hang out with me anymore; they took me aside one day at recess to tell me this, emphasizing how annoyingly needy I'd become. I started spending my lunches and recesses alone, sitting in a corner and reading a book.

My cousin, who was fifteen that year, sensed how unhappy I was and taught me her favourite prayer. She said that whenever she felt that life was unbearable, she would bow her head and beg God to put her out of her misery. That way, she said, she wasn't *really* asking to die, which is, of course, a sin – she was just asking God to choose whatever He felt was the best solution to her problems. I was captivated by this idea.

The fact was that my family had never been particularly religious. In fact, my father was an atheist and would gladly debate anyone on the existence of God. And although my mother had made sure to have my sisters and I baptized and managed to drag us to church on a fairly regular basis, we didn't really talk about God or sin or anything like that except in a curiously detached, anthropological sort of way. There was never any mention of saying prayers at bedtime or mealtimes; in fact, the only time we ever prayed was when we said grace over Christmas or Easter dinner.

After that conversation with my cousin, though, I started praying. I would get down on my knees by my bed every night, just like they did in books and movies, and I would beg God to either make things better or else let me die.

8.

By the age of sixteen, I was crying all the time. At school, I would dash off to the washroom and sob in one of the stalls, or else I would just sit there in the hallway and let the tears drip down my face. At home I would lock myself in my bedroom, coming out only to eat or use the bathroom. I couldn't sleep at night, and would get up and play my ten year old sister's stupid, babyish computer games for hours on end. During the day, I was exhausted, and would often fall asleep during class. I bored all of my friends with lengthy descriptions of my romantic troubles, spending hours hashing and rehashing conversations I'd had with the boys that I liked. I couldn't concentrate in class and only managed to absorb a fraction of what was being taught. I stopped caring about my marks; over the course of tenth grade I went from being on the honour roll to barely pulling Cs and Ds. No one really seemed to notice though – or if they did, they just told me that I'd better pull my socks up if I wanted to get into university.

Over all of this was stretched a grey pall of grinding hopelessness. I wasn't going anywhere. I wasn't loved by anyone. I wasn't talented in the way that my friends were. I was smart, but I couldn't translate that into good grades anymore. All that I wanted was to get out of Kitchener, but I wasn't even sure that I could manage to do that anymore.

I finally broke down and told my mother how miserable I was, and she made me an appointment with our family doctor. I went by myself, taking the bus across town after school one day, and told him that I thought I was depressed. He peered into my face and said that yes, I did look like I was feeling pretty blue. He wrote me a prescription for Paxil and referred me to a therapist. That was it – no real inquiries into what was happening in my life, no blood tests to rule out anything physical, no nothing – just an old man in a crisp white jacket telling me that I looked sad.

Not knowing what else to do, I took the pills and went to see the therapist. He was another old man, and he laughed when he read my intake form. On it, I'd written that I was "jaded and cynical," thinking that those terms made me sound intelligent and grown up.

He'd thought that I'd meant it as a joke.

I only saw him twice.

The Paxil didn't really seem to do much, so my doctor switched me to Prozac. That didn't seem to do much either, but my doctor said that we should just try increasing it, because maybe we hadn't found the right dosage yet. Over the course of the next two years, right up until I moved to Halifax, he just kept nudging the number of milligrams I took every day higher and higher. When I told him that the medication was making me feel awful, he told me that it was my best hope and then slyly asked how therapy was going. I knew that I was beaten. Eventually, I learned to keep my mouth shut when he asked me how I was feeling; I had lost all faith in his ability to fix me.

I kept taking those glossy little green and white pills, even though I was sure that they weren't doing any good. They were a sort of talisman, something that I could throw in people's faces when they accused me of malingering or not trying hard enough to get better.

"I'm taking Prozac," I would say.

This was in Prozac's heyday, and the name alone was enough to make an impact.

"I'm doing the best that I can."

And maybe I wasn't, but I felt like I was.

9.

I like to refer to 2003 as my annus horribilis.

I prefer this term for a variety of reasons:

a) It's Latin, which is classy

b) Queen Elizabeth II once used it, which makes it double classy

c) Annus looks/sounds like anus, and I am a twelve year old boy

There are a variety of reasons why 2003 was such a terrible year. My ever-present financial problems had finally achieved critical mass, meaning that I wasn't able to complete what would have been the third and likely final year of my bachelor of arts. Not only that, but I owed everyone and everything money, a fact that led to a bad falling out with my best friend. In the spring of 2003 I'd auditioned for the second time to get into Dalhousie's theatre program, and had been summarily rejected once again.

The straw that finally broke the camel's back was the fact that I'd somehow fallen in love with my friend Stephen in February of that year. Fallen isn't quite the word I want, though, even if it does contain the right idea of hurtling through something towards an unknown place. But the sense of falling, especially falling in love, is usually supposed to be pleasant. It's the moment when you jump off that cliff and give yourself over to something bigger, like the force of gravity or the magnetic pull of someone else's heart. It should be a scary, sure, but also exhilarating. It should be at least somewhat fun.

Being in love with Stephen was never fun, though. Not for me. Not during the weeks I spent pining over him, analyzing and re-analyzing our every interaction. Not even when I found out that he felt the same way about me. I couldn't ever give myself over to love or happiness or exhilaration – the only thing I could ever give myself over to was fear.

So maybe, instead of *falling*, I'll say that I crashed into love, awkwardly and painfully.

On Valentine's Day, of all days.

My roommates and I had invited all of our friends over for what we ironically termed our Anti-Valentine's Party. The soirée had started out, in typical Maritime fashion, with everyone gathered in the kitchen, and then eventually disintegrated into several smaller groups scattered around our apartment, including but not limited to a joint-rolling tutorial in my bedroom, a cheap drunk of a girl, attended by a few sympathetic ladies-in-waiting, vomiting red wine all over our bathtub, and several friends snorting coke off my roommate's bedside table. Stephen, who was in the same program at school as several of my friends, was staying over because he lived out of town. The plan had been for him to sleep in the living room, but when the red-wine-vomit girl declared that she couldn't make it home, Stephen gallantly offered her the couch and then took me up on my invitation to sleep on my bedroom floor. Except that neither of us slept – we stayed up all night, talking about all the stupid ephemera that seems so important at the beginning of a relationship. According to my journal, the topics of discussion included: *"... post-apocalyptic visions of the world, the Tunguska event, volcanoes, mass extinctions, Greek mythology, the coming war, a room with walls made entirely of drawers, Atlantis, colonizing the moon, the perfect mattress."*

The air in my room, lit only by a chain of small pink paper lanterns that I'd hung along one wall, was hazy with pot smoke and incense. I remember sitting there, this ratty old blue fleece blanket wrapped around my shoulders, animatedly jumping from one subject to another. It was one of those times when every wheel and cog in the universe seems to suddenly find its groove and they all begin move in perfect synchronization. My heart was pounding, and I couldn't keep my hands still as I tried to outline some concept or another for him. There was a funny tingling all over my skin, like I was on the edge of something very big and important. It felt like magic: wild, dangerous magic.

I was so in love with him.

So unbearably in love.

It ended, of course. It ended about three months after it began, and it ended in total, devastating heartbreak. I was sick with grief. I'd never really before understood the pathology of a broken heart; I'd always thought that the term was purely emotional. But the spot where I imagined my heart to be literally hurt; my chest ached with sadness, and I felt like I couldn't breathe.

In the weeks that followed, everything seemed like a chore. Even mundane, day-to-day activities were overwhelming, so I did as few of them as possible; I didn't get dressed in the morning, I didn't cook any meals, and I didn't shower or brush my teeth. Instead I slept all day, read sad books, and occasionally ate packets of instant oatmeal.

I started calling my best friend several times a day, forcing her to listen to my stupid robot voice dissect my failed relationship over and over again. I couldn't talk about anything else; no other subject held any interest for me. Every phone call ended with me tearfully asking if she thought that we might ever get back together. My best friend, bless her heart, dutifully replied every single time that she was sure that we would.

Crying became my main state of being. In the mornings, after my roommates left for work, I would drag myself to the kitchen and sit there, in my bathrobe, crying over my toast and coffee. I would cry while I showered, or else cry while sitting on our bright floral couch. Sometimes, just to change things up, I would haul open the living room window, pull out the screen, and crawl out onto the roof of the porch so that I could cry outside without actually having to leave the house. When I couldn't cry anymore, I would just lie there, letting myself fill up with my sick, bloated grief until it threatened to spill out of me all over again. And then I would cry some more.

It wasn't just that I'd loved Stephen – not that I used the word *love* back then; none of us did – it was also that I was afraid that I would never feel that same attraction for anyone else, ever.

I might have been a late bloomer anyway when it came to sex, but the fact that I'd been put on anti-depressants while still in my mid-teens had done my libido absolutely no favours. I mean, seriously, if you ever wanted to fuck up a teenager's sex life, give them a prescription for an SSRI. It killed every single pleasure cell inside of me.

I was incapable of any kind of sexual feeling. When people said that they were horny, I honestly had no idea what they meant. I kissed boys, of course, and sometimes went further than that, but none of it produced any kind of reaction in me. It just felt like warm, rubbery skin touching skin, which wasn't exactly *un*pleasant, but also wasn't the be-all-and-end-all that my friends made it out to be. It wasn't, for example, as fun or satisfying as reading a really good book.

But still, I kissed and touched and more because the boys liked it, and I wanted them to like me. And doing all of those things (things which were, admittedly, usually over fairly quickly) meant that we could get to the stuff that I liked – the holding each other, the whispering in the dark, the showing of scars and the telling of secrets.

With Stephen, though, it was different. He was the first person that I'd ever felt any kind of physical attraction to, a fact that frankly terrified me. It terrified me when we were together, because my body was suddenly, painfully wide awake, and it terrified me after we broke up, because I thought that I would never meet anyone who made me feel like that ever again.

My breakup with Stephen neatly marked the beginning of the second major depressive episode in my life. In retrospect, I think that it might have gone easier for me if I'd been self-aware enough to realize that my devastation was at least partly chemically-induced. Instead, I honestly thought that I was pathetically losing my shit over the end of a three month relationship. So not only was I pretty fucking sad, but I was also deeply embarrassed and angry with myself for how sad I felt. I didn't understand why I couldn't get my life together, and I bought into the old lie that it was somehow the result of laziness or a lack of willpower.

See, this is the tricky thing about depression and the lies that it tells you – it masquerades itself so brilliantly as your own clear, undiseased thoughts that you can very rarely, if ever, catch it in the act of lying. It's only later, once you're healthier and finally able to sift through all of the sweet nothings your sadness has been whispering to you these many weeks and months, that you can begin to separate the truths from the untruths. When you're in the thick of it, though, your mind turns traitor and offers you the worst advice possible, the main result of which is that you feel worse and worse and worse; it's like you're inhabited by one of those weird parasites that forces you to do things that you wouldn't normally do in order to ensure its own survival. Because your depression wants so badly to survive. All of which is to say that instead of recognizing my depression for what it was, instead of admitting that things were quickly spiralling of control and insisting that I get some kind of help, my sick brain instead told me that everything was my fault. The breakup was my fault. My inability to get over it was my fault. My malingering sadness was especially my fault.

My depression pretended to love me. It sweetly explained that it was my only real friend, and showed me, presenting very strong and compelling evidence, that everyone else thought that I was pathetic. Hadn't I noticed, it wondered, that a silence descended whenever I entered a room and laughter erupted when I left? Hadn't it occurred to me that no one had ever really loved me, that they'd only ever loved my friendliness, my readiness to help, my sympathetic ear? Hadn't I realized yet how very lonely and unpopular I was? My ailing mind lied to me over and over again, and I swallowed each untruth the way that a man lost in a desert will frantically gulp down even the warmest, most foul-tasting water. Those lies were the only sustenance that I had.

Stephen and I broke up in April, and I remember being so cold all through that spring and summer, even when the temperature rose to the mid-30s in July and August. I wore sweaters and long-sleeved shirts constantly; the sun, no matter how bright, couldn't seem to touch me. Whenever I had to be around others I tried to act normally, but I felt as if I'd forgotten how to show any emotion beyond that sick, gutted sadness. I would try to fake a smile if I thought that social codes demanded one, my lips stretching apart into a wavering grimace, but I could tell by the looks on other people's faces that I was badly missing the mark. I lost weight, and yet, in complete contradiction to this fact, my body felt heavy and numb, my skin as cold and dead as a snake's. My joints ached and I felt as if my bones were made of glass, clinking together painfully with every step. Things that I'd once been able to do without any measurable effort, like forming a thought or following a conversation or opening my mouth to speak, became unbearably difficult. I drifted ghost-like through my days, my eyes dull and my mouth full of ash.

I thought that something must eventually happen, because I couldn't imagine going on living like this, but I couldn't figure out what that something might be. I knew that I had to make a change, but I didn't know what that change was, and so I had no idea where to start.

I'd meant to stay in Halifax for the whole summer, but things were so bad that my mother convinced me to come home. Except that she didn't exactly live at *home* anymore – she'd moved less than a year earlier to Kingston, Ontario, four hours away from where I'd grown up and gone to high school, so it wasn't even as if I was going back to a place where I had a support network of old friends. The only people that I knew in Kingston were my mother, my sisters and my aunt and uncle. And while it was nice to have my mother cook and clean and care for me, being isolated in that way made me feel even worse that I already did. I spent my days crying on her pull-out couch, calling each of my Halifax friends in turn and obsessively checking my email to see if Stephen had sent me anything.

My mother tried to cheer me up by planning family trips to Ottawa and Montreal, or by taking us all out to the movies or for ice cream. Whenever she did this, she would look at me expectantly to see if her plan had worked, but it never had. No matter what I did, no matter what anyone did, I couldn't be shaken out of my gloom. And every time she looked at me in this way, I felt even worse, because I knew how hard she was trying to make me happy. She was spending money she didn't have, money that should have gone towards new school clothes or books or fun activities for my sisters, and the guilt of that knowledge sat heavy in my chest. But even that guilt couldn't make me pull myself together.

To make matters worse, I couldn't find a job in Kingston, so I had no way of paying for my apartment back in Halifax. Over the course of the past year, there had been several times when I hadn't been able to make rent, and my roommate's parents had very generously covered my portion. Every time they did this, I would, in a fit of shame and panic, assure them that I'd pay them back as soon as I could; I failed to mention, of course, that I wasn't sure when I would ever be able to do that. I knew that it was only a matter of time before they put their collective parental foot down about our living situation, and apparently my lack of summer employment was a bridge too far.

My friends' parents told her that she could no longer live with me. Since they paid for all of her rent, tuition and groceries, she had no choice but to go along with what they said. Her parents were completely in the right, of course, and I would have done the same if I had been in their position, but still, I was devastated.

Angry, ashamed, and devastated.

And as awful as Kingston was, it was still something of a reprieve from the worst of my sadness; I dreaded going back to Halifax and facing all of the problems I'd tried run away from. But I did, because I saw no alternative. Stepping off the train on that September afternoon, the air thick and humid with early-autumn haze, I was suddenly right back where I'd been two months earlier. It was as if everything and everyone there had been in suspended animation, waiting for me to get back; nothing felt any different than it had been when I'd left, except that now I was living with a total stranger instead of my closest friends.

My situation grew even grimmer as the month passed. I tried going to classes for a few weeks, hoping that I'd be able to sort out my money situation, but it was impossible. I talked to everyone at the school that I could think of, and each of them said that there was nothing *they* could do, but had I considered talking to so-and-so? When I told them that it was so-and-so who'd suggested that I come to *them*, they would just shrug their shoulders apologetically. None of them seemed to understand that they were ruining my whole stupid life; what did they care? There were other students, paying students and therefore more important students, who needed their attention. They were running a business, I was just another number in their system, and I was no longer profitable. End of story.

So I went to each of my professors in turn and told them that I had to leave school. My favourite teacher, Doctor O'Connor, was outraged on my behalf, and said that it made no sense for someone who was bright, capable and dying to learn to be barred from getting an education. Unfortunately, he had no concrete suggestions of what I could do; he just asked if I could keep attending classes while I tried to figure things out. I couldn't, though – I needed to get a job, soon, or else I wouldn't be able to pay my rent.

I started crying, hard, while I was in his office, and he silently passed me his handkerchief. Afterwards, as I was leaving, I tried to give the tear-strained, snot-covered square of cloth back to him, but he told me to go ahead and keep it. For some reason that one stupid little act really touched me; like, here was this very clean, handsome, well-dressed man faced with this miserable, disheveled girl, and he very kindly gives her his beautifully white handkerchief. It was like something out of a book, and I thought that if I could maybe resemble an interesting character in an interesting book, then some amazing plot twist might conceivably come along and save me.

I kept that handkerchief and still have it today, though I'm not sure why; it's sort of a symbol, I guess, for something that I don't fully understand. Maybe what really got me was the fact that, out of everyone that I talked to at that huge, old brick school that had been my home for the past two years, he was the only one who seemed to think that I was worth anything beyond whether or not I was able to pay tuition. He saw that I was smart, and he knew that I wanted to learn, and he cared about that. In that whole dark month of September, Doctor O'Connor giving me his handkerchief might very well have been the brightest spot.

After formally leaving school, I started to look for a job, although I really had no idea what I wanted to do. Scratch that, I didn't even know what I *could* do. What types of jobs did people with half a degree have? So I printed up a stack of resumes and started handing them out everywhere – bookstores, clothing stores, fancy restaurants, fast food restaurants, nannying agencies, gas stations. I pored over the want-ads and called people who were looking for, well, anything. No one seemed to be hiring, though; I don't know if it was the chronically-awful maritime economy or the off-putting nature of my general, disquieting misery, but I couldn't find anything.

Of course, there's also the possibility that my hunt for work wasn't as diligent as I remember. It's likely that I only spent one or two lacklustre afternoons passing out resumes at the mall before giving up completely. Although I felt like I was out there, pounding the pavement and looking for a job, chances are that I spent most of my time sitting on my front stoop, reading dog-eared favourites and drinking cup after cup of coffee. It's not that I was especially lazy, or at least not lazy in the classical sense of the word; it's just that I lived in a chronic state of bleak exhaustion. Part of that was the energy-sapping weight of my sadness, and part of it was that over the summer, my mother's doctor in Kingston had put me on this drug that was supposed to be both anti-depressant and sleeping pill, with the result that I slept fourteen (broken) hours a night and was groggy all day long. I continued to take it, though, even though it didn't really improve my mood or fix my sleep problems in a way that made me able to function.

I did finally find part-time work – and by part-time I mean approximately ten hours a week –

babysitting a twelve-year-old boy named Joey who had Asperger Syndrome. I wanted the job so badly that I told his mother that I was still a student, even though by that time I patently wasn't, because I was afraid that she would find it strange for someone who wasn't in school to want a job with so few hours. But the truth was that this job was the only one I'd even been offered an interview for, and even a cheque for eighty dollars a week was better than nothing.

I spent my first month back in Halifax scrabbling to be able to maintain some kind of foothold on what felt like a rapidly shifting foundation. Meanwhile, my friends went on with their ordinary school lives around me – classes and parties and tutorials and rehearsals. Backpacks stuffed with huge, thick textbooks and Sunday morning hangovers and late-night study sessions over cup after cup of vile, gut-rotting coffee. Trips to the labyrinthine Killam library, where you could easily spend hours getting lost in the stacks. Fretting over what to wear to the bar, and whether your makeup was over-the-top or exactly right. Kissing strangers and kissing old friends and falling in love and falling out of love. I missed all of it, even the stuff that I'd hated, even the stuff that had made me feel awful.

That type of awful was so much better than the grinding grey sadness I lived in that September.

I missed my friends, but if I was being honest with myself, I wasn't even sure if they *were* still my friends. If I was this unbearable to myself, then how much worse must I seem to the people around me? So I started trying to avoid them, which was easy because they all lived up near the school, while I was stranded in Halifax's North End. When my friends called, I refused to answer the phone. When I heard their voices on the porch, heard them knock on the door, I would hide in my bedroom until they left. They would leave messages on my voicemail, which I would listen to and then delete. Sometimes they left notes in my mailbox, which I would cry bitterly over and then hide in a shoebox in my closet.

I felt that I was doing them a favour by staying out of their way. I was sure that they were only calling or visiting me out of a misplaced feeling of obligation, and that by not answering the phone or door I was somehow relieving them of the burden of me. I didn't fit into their neatly-ordered campus world anymore; they were all still busy-bee students, while I had become the working poor. We weren't the same species anymore, and it was better if we cut our ties cleanly rather than drag everything out.

I did go to one party with some of my old friends, once. I'm not even sure, now, how I was talked into it. It was at the enormous, dilapidated old house where Stephen was living with five other people, and certainly his presence was part of the reason why I went. I knew, I mean, I empirically *knew*, that going to that party was a bad idea, but still, I couldn't stay away. I remember feeling this dread over the idea of seeing him, but at the same time very much wanting to be around him – that funny double-feeling that you get around someone you love who doesn't love you back.

So I went to the party, and I put on a brave face when I saw Stephen. I tried not to feel hurt when he quickly turned away after exchanging only a few brief, friendly words with me. I sat in the living room, which stank of beer and pot and that strange, pleasantly sweaty smell that belongs especially to boys in their teens and early twenties. People handed me plastic cups full of fizzy stuff which I drank without question. My cheeks began to flush, and everything I said and did took on a feverish quality; I talked animatedly, hoping that I was being funny and charming. At one point, Stephen's friend Malcolm and I sang a funny little version of the Ben Folds song Army, with me chiming in as the horn section. I laughed, maybe too loudly, and smiled, maybe a little too widely. I did a mostly passable imitation of a normal person who lives in the person-world and does person-things. Whenever Stephen would come into a room, I would look at him, but then quickly look away; I did my best to tuck my heartbreak away somewhere where no one would be able to sniff it out. For a little while, at least, I felt like I was succeeding at holding everything together.

It wasn't long, though, before everything started grating on me. The noise was too loud, the people too drunk, the lights too bright. I felt my façade starting to slip, felt that old familiar sting in my eyes, and I knew that the fairy godmother's coach was about to turn back into a pumpkin. I knew that I should just go home, but instead I went upstairs, thinking that I could take a short break and come back to the party when I felt better.

I went upstairs and found Stephen sprawled out on the floor of his room. So I sprawled out next to him and we talked for a while, and just that simple fact made me so happy. Eventually he got up, saying that he wanted to make the rounds of the party and tell everyone goodnight before he passed out. After he left, I sat with my back against his bed, pressed my face against my bent knees and started to cry. I couldn't help it – it was like one of those times when you suddenly realize that you're going to be sick, except that instead of throwing up, I let myself dissolve into a soggy, tearstained mess.

Why did I cry in Stephen's room? Why didn't I run to the bathroom, or someone else's bedroom, or hightail it down the stairs and out the door?

Here are the reasons that I told myself at the time: I'd thought that he would be gone for at least a solid half hour, and I didn't want to embarrass myself in front of his roommates, and I hoped that I could just get it out of my system and somehow keep my pathetically threadbare dignity intact.

Here's what was almost certainly the real reason: I wanted Stephen to find me. I wanted him to find me and comfort me because I loved him and I missed him and goddamnit I was so fucking sad and lonely.

He did find me, of course. He ended up only being gone for a few minutes, and when he came back I was mid-sob, my face all squinched up and covered in snot. Then, according to my journal, this happened:

He came right over to me and said, "Hey, are you ok? What's wrong?" in his oh-so-sweet 'I'm such a nice guy' voice. He wrapped his arms around me and lay down on the bed, so that I was sitting on the floor with the upper half of my body sprawled across his chest.

He was so nice, gently rubbing my back, fiddling with the strap of my tank top and stroking me with his fingertips. Somehow, we ended up holding hands with our fingers interlaced together, his other arm around me and my face pressed against his chest. I was sobbing and telling him all the things that I'd been worrying about – school, money, everybody hating me, how I feel so invisible – all the things I've been feeling so miserable about lately. And he listened and told me to do whatever it was that made me happy, and screw everyone else.

When I got up, I realized that there was a big black mascara-y smudge from where I'd been crying on the front of his t-shirt. I apologized profusely – I'd been apologizing the whole time I'd been crying, I felt so bad that he'd had to deal with me. He said not to worry abut it, the shirt had to be washed anyway.

He looked really out of it, and started hinting that he wanted to sleep. I stayed a few more minutes – maybe a few too many, but I was exhausted, too, and had actually fallen asleep on him at one point. We hugged a couple more times and then I left – but not before a few of his roommates and friends had seen us holding each other.

By the next afternoon, everyone, and I mean everyone, knew all about how I had drunkenly thrown myself at Stephen. Living in Halifax is like playing a lifelong game of telephone – whenever you do something, it's only a matter of hours before the rest of the city knows at least a distorted version of your business.

Was I drunkenly throwing myself at Stephen? Maybe. Probably. I'm not sure that throwing is the word I would use, but for sure when he started holding me and rubbing my back, there was this quiet moment of, *maybe this is my chance to get him back.*

How fucking embarrassing, how stereotypically female, to try to seduce someone by making them pity you.

How sickening to have everyone find out what you've done, and then laugh at you for it.

The worst of it came when I met up for coffee with one of Stephen's roommates, a girl named Kate, the day after the party. She told me that he'd spent the morning loudly complaining about what had happened. He was annoyed that my makeup had stained his shirt, she said, and irritated that I'd kept him awake with my crying when all he'd wanted to do was fall asleep.

"But that's not really what happened!" I exclaimed, starting to panic. "That's not what happened at all."

Kate just shrugged sympathetically.

"I'm not sure that you can convince anyone of that now. Anyway, everyone'll forget soon enough."

But I didn't think that they'd forget. I thought that all of my friends and acquaintances would just add this latest shame to the long list of Reasons To Hate Anne that they'd been composing the entire time that they'd known me.

The rest of September passed in a blur of soggy dead leaves and raw grey skies. I babysat for a few hours each afternoon, but other than that my days were empty. I wonder, now, what I did with all of those free hours. I read a lot, I think, digging out old favourites like *The Lion, the Witch and the Wardrobe* and *Harry Potter*; the sort of books that are like comfort food for the soul. I spent a lot of time on my roommate's computer, either posting on the Tori Amos message board that I helped moderate or else playing mindless games while listening to sad music. I walked around my new neighbourhood, reciting the names of the streets to myself like a rhyme: Gottingen, Agricola, Creighton, Cunard, Falkland, Maitland. I went down to the harbour and stood out on the end of one of the wharves, staring out into the bleak watery nothing.

In my journal I wrote:

I'm lonely here, and I'm not tough enough for this neighbourhood – they can see right through my translucent skin to my uncertain heart.

I couldn't stop thinking about what had happened with Stephen at that party; I worried at it like a dog with a bone. I spent my days alternating between being indignantly angry with him over what he'd said and done and just wanting to discover whatever the secret was to making him love me again. If he'd ever loved me. Which was doubtful.

At some point, I scraped together enough courage to call him and ask him out for coffee. I thought that if I explained why I was so angry and hurt, then maybe he would see how bad things were for me and throw me a bone by way of an apology or a little bit of kindness. At that point, even just a hug or a smile or a gentle word would have gone a long way. I wanted something, anything from him to prove that I wasn't a complete pathetic failure as a human being.

Surprisingly, Stephen agreed right away to coffee. We set a date – the afternoon of Sunday, September 28th at the Coburg Coffee House. I didn't know what he was expecting, or if he had any idea about why I wanted to see him, but I was hoping to catch him off-guard. I figured that if I couldn't have talent or beauty or love on my side, at the very least I would have the element of surprise. For some reason this was very important to me.

September 28th came, and I spent the morning in a bundle of raw nerves. What was I going to say? What was I going to wear? What would I do if he got angry and told me that he never wanted to see me again? I was so occupied with these thoughts that I failed to notice that the sky outside was growing darker and grimmer, and I didn't hear the sharp, mean wind that was picking up and tossing the trees hard against the side of the house.

It wasn't until my mother called sometime mid-afternoon and asked if we were ready for the coming hurricane that I realized what was happening. Shortly after that, the power went out, and I spent an hour playing solitaire on my roommate's computer until the battery died.

I thought about calling Stephen and cancelling our meeting, but I decided that he could figure out that it wasn't going to happen all on his own.

Anyway, I got a few minutes' satisfaction out of picturing him going to the Coburg and waiting for me in the middle of the howling storm; even thought I realized how incredibly unlikely this scenario was, I felt meanly glad. Let him think he'd been stood up, I thought. Let *him* know for once what it felt like to be alone and forgotten.

And anyway, not long after that, the phone lines went down, so I couldn't have called him even if I'd wanted to.

Hurricane Juan hit Halifax hard, a fact that I was strangely thrilled about. The storm shook me out of my gloom, in the way that wild weather almost always does. There's this sense of potential at times like that, as if anything could happen; the air feels charged, electric, in a way that makes my heart swell with excitement. It's like I'm standing on the brink of something world-changing, like the old order could be entirely wiped out and I might wake up in the morning to a whole new life.

I went out into the storm that night and walked around the deserted city. The wind was blowing so hard that it knocked me with enough force to tear the straps on my flip flops, but I didn't care. I just went barefoot. I made my way down to the waterfront, where huge waves were already violently dismantling the piers and crashing up onto the boardwalk. I stood by the water's edge and let the waves smash over me. I loved their strength, the way they tasted of cold, raw power.

I loved standing there and facing up to something much bigger than I was, something with the power to destroy cities. I wasn't afraid; I knew that I was more than a match for this storm.

Later, the police found me wandering through the glass catwalks that connected the Delta Barrington Hotel to Scotia Square Mall. They gave me a lecture about how dangerous it was to be there, told me what a huge risk there was of the wind shattering the glass, then walked me down to the street and watched as I made my way up Cogswell. They treated me like a stupid little kid, but I didn't care. I'd tasted something new that night, and I felt changed. I only hoped that the change would last.

When I got home, I made myself a little makeshift bed on the floor of our kitchen, the only windowless room in our apartment. The threat of flying glass hadn't frightened me when I was downtown, but now that I was warm and dry and safe, I felt weaker, diminished. I lay awake late into the night listening to the sounds of Hurricane Juan – the debris driven hard into the walls of our building, the groaning of trees being uprooted, and the sound of shattering glass and splintering wood as houses up and down the street sighed and gave themselves up to the storm.

The morning after Juan was beautiful, sunny and warm. It didn't feel like a fresh start, though. It felt like my city had been as torn up as my heart, and, like me, Halifax had to slowly dig itself out of this mess and keep going as best as it could.

The city, lost somewhere under a tangle of mangled branches, dead trees and downed power lines, shut down in the week following the hurricane. We were all of us living in the dark, enduring cold showers and other daily miseries, while we waited for the electricity to come back. A state of emergency was declared and we watched, bemused, as the army rolled in to put our city back together. Our lives a funny sort of holiday feeling; nobody had to work or go to school, so my friends and I spent our days on each other's porches drinking cheap rum mixed with fruit juice. Because we couldn't use our stoves or any other appliances, we barbecued everything; we even barbecued a pot pie by wrapping it in tinfoil. We stayed up late into the night, playing cards by candlelight or just hanging out and talking.

For the first time since coming back to Halifax, I felt relatively normal. For that one week, my friends weren't students, and I wasn't an underemployed failure; we were all just a bunch of people trying to get through a tricky time. We all looked out for each other that week as we learned to navigate our post-hurricane city, and suddenly I felt like other people might actually care about my safety and well-being. I started to feel a little bit hopeful. I thought, *If only things could be like this forever.*

They couldn't, of course. Eventually the power came back on, schools and businesses opened their doors again, and everyone went back to their regular lives. I would have, too, except that I didn't have a regular life to go back to. So instead I dove back into my bed and, as the city started to dazedly shake itself out of its stupor, I lay there and waited while all of my bad feelings came slowly creeping back. Like some kind of exotic parasite, they wriggled their way into my brain; but whereas tapeworms and their ilk will eat up all of the delicious calories that you've consumed and leave you to starve, my own special brand of worm ate up any good thoughts that I might have and left me wanting to die.

I was in a funny sort of limbo in those days; I felt like I had no place in the land of the living, but didn't have the bravery or dedication necessary to make my way to the land of the dead. I knew that I had to commit to one or the other, but I couldn't, or maybe just wouldn't. Living seemed like far too much effort with too little return, like putting coin after coin into an arcade game only to win some useless plastic trinket as my prize. And death – well, death was still too enormous, too much of a seething, formless void to fully consider. Sure, I might daydream about it, might even write *I want to die* over and over in my journal, but I didn't really mean that. Did I?

So I did my pathetic best to survive, even if that best wasn't terribly useful or good. I took my pills every day. I saw my therapist, Denise, at least once, sometimes twice a week, even though she drove me up the wall with her endless parade of patronizing comments and suggestions.

I saw my doctor nearly as often as I saw Denise; as the autumn wore on, he grew increasingly concerned, and had me come in to see him on a weekly basis. The medication that I was on, those antidepressant-slash-sleeping-pills, didn't seem to be helping, so he increased my dosage, and then increased it again. When that didn't do anything, he switched me to a different medication, but that one didn't seem to help either. At every appointment, he would ask if my mood was any better, and every time I would duck my head and mutter that I felt exactly the same. He always seemed deeply disappointed, as if he'd been sure that *this* time he'd managed to fix the problem. I thought that if I were an easier, more cooperative patient, that he would be able to cure me, but I wasn't, so he couldn't. Even my lack of recovery was probably somehow my own fault.

I hated being such a constant source of disappointment to him.

By mid-October, instead of getting better, I was getting worse. Without my sleeping pills, my insomnia was back in full force; most nights I wouldn't begin to drift until the sky was lightening into another damp, grey Halifax morning. When I did sleep, I had gasping, bone-rattling nightmares. My chest felt tight all the time, as if I was wearing a corset and someone was slowly pulling on the ties. Everything, even totally normal, everyday things like checking my email or deciding what to eat, made me feel panicked. My hands shook. My voice shook. A sick, stinking pit opened up in my stomach, and I could taste bile in my throat whenever I opened my mouth to speak.

When I told all of this to my doctor, he gave me a diagnosis of generalized anxiety disorder to go along with my my previously-earned diagnosis of dysthymia (which is really just a fancy way of saying "feeling pretty sad most of the time"). Instead of finding comfort in the fact that all of my newer symptoms could be rounded up, bundled together and neatly covered by one catch-all label, I felt myself growing even more anxious. Instead of being happy that what I was feeling was identifiable and, hopefully, treatable, I felt deeply uneasy. I couldn't help but wonder what else lay dormant in me – some kind of personality disorder? Latent schizophrenia? A good old fashioned psychotic break? There was no way of knowing what other little ticking time bombs were nestled deep in my brain.

Anxiety is exhausting. It feels like your mind is doing line after line of coke, with barely a pause in between. Your thoughts, which are almost always basic variations on the same theme, race frantically. Even just deciding what to wear or whether or not you should shower makes you feel as if you've run a marathon. At night, my anxious thoughts were amplified in the silent dark, which meant that even when my body was bone-fucking-tired I still couldn't sleep. Instead, I stayed awake playing old conversations over and over in my head, trying to figure out what I should have said or done differently. It wasn't as if I wanted, or even intended, to do this; it just kept happening, night after night, and I didn't know how to stop it.

In an effort to try to shut my thoughts off, I started taking over-the-counter sleeping pills. At first they were great – within half an hour of taking one, I would start to feel a funny warmth creeping up along my limbs, and my body would start to feel slow and heavy. I would crash onto my bed and sleep would wash over me like a wave, drawing me off somewhere to float gently along until morning. Unfortunately, the pills only worked for a week, maybe a week and a half – after that my body's tolerance for them increased to the point where they lost almost all effectiveness. Except it was even worse than before I'd started taking the pills, because now I needed those bright, hard red capsules to achieve even the pathetic amount of sleep I'd been getting back when I wasn't taking any medication. Without the pills, I suddenly couldn't sleep at all.

There's a very good reason why sleep deprivation is used as a form of torture, and lack of sleep made me feel even more unhinged than before. When I washed the dishes, I would stop cold in the middle of wiping down a sharp knife and stare at it, wondering what would happen if the hand holding the knife suddenly took on a life of its own. When I crossed the street, I would imagine that I'd been hit by a car, and that I was now a ghost walking away from my body. The world seemed to be full of little more than opportunities to die, and death, with it's cold, hard nothingness, became more and more appealing. And whereas these thoughts would have concerned, even frightened me a few weeks earlier, now they seemed like the most comforting things that I had.

But still, I kept trying to find my way back to some kind of safer, higher ground. I kept telling myself that if only I could find a way to sleep, then things would be better.

So I kept taking the sleeping pills, with the result that I slept less and less.

I called the sleeping pill manufacturer's twenty four hour hotline late one night, desperate for unconsciousness, and asked – begged, really – to know if it was all right to take two pills. Just one pill wasn't working anymore, I explained, and I was so tired that I couldn't function.

"I can't advise you to take more than one pill," the girl on the other end of the line said brightly, "but I'll tell you what I can do! I'll send you a free box of pills, because it's entirely possible that they're not working because you got a bad batch."

I wanted to explain to her that I'd been taking the damn pills every night for two and a half weeks, and my lack of sleep had nothing to do with a "bad batch" and everything to do with my increasing tolerance for over-the-counter tranquilizers, but I wasn't sure that I had the ability to string all of that together into any kind of grammatically-sound sentence. And, I mean – hey, free pills! Who was I to look a gift horse like that in the mouth? So I gave her my address, and that night I drank a glass of wine with my sleeping pill. Those two things in combination gave me that same dizzy, drowsy, heavy feeling, although I had a bad headache in the morning.

I thought, This is why they tell you not to mix sleeping pills with alcohol.

I thought, I should be careful not to do that again.

But I did, of course; I just kept a glass of water and a bottle of Tylenol on my bedside table to kill the headache I now had every morning.

The sleeping pills and wine were a way of testing myself, seeing how far I could or would go towards the edge before pulling myself back. It was for that same reason that I started cutting myself. I would do this nearly every evening, while my law student roommate was out doing whatever it is law student roommates do.

There was a whole ritual to the cutting. First, I would put something comforting and familiar on the television, like M*A*S*H or Star Trek. I would set up a little station for myself on the couch, complete with a pair of sharp kitchen scissors and a stack of paper towels. I would sit there for a while, watching my show and screwing up my courage, and then I would pick up the scissors and I would cut chunks out of my flesh. Actual, sizeable chunks.

I focused mainly on my wrists, but when those became too torn up I started cutting my upper arm, and then my inner thighs and my soft, flabby belly. In the shower I would take my razor and slash at myself, mostly obeying what I called the "bathing suit rule" – which meant not cutting anything (other than my wrists, I guess) that wouldn't be covered by a bathing suit. I didn't want to get caught, after all. This wasn't a cry for help.

Since then, I've read a lot about cutting and why people do it, and the general consensus seems to be that it helps relieve emotional tension. Maybe that's true for some people, and maybe it's even true to a certain extent for me, but what I really got out of it was a sort of steadiness that I'd been missing. When I cut myself, that took all of my focus, and somehow that stopped my hands from shaking. While I was cutting, I was so absorbed in what I was doing that I couldn't think about anything else. Cutting made my mind go deliciously blank, and that blankness stayed with me for a few hours afterwards. And cutting was something that was mine, and mine only – no one else, not even Denise, knew about it. As I walked around during the day and my cuts stung beneath my layers of clothing, it felt nice, somehow, to have a secret.

My other secret was that I had timed and mapped out my walk to go pick up Joey so that it happened right around when Stephen was walking home from class. This wasn't exactly difficult; Stephen's classes ended for the day right around when Joey's school let out, and the school itself was only a block away from the university campus. And anyway, I'd run into him a few times without even trying; really, I was just sort of arranging things so as to facilitate what already had a fairly high chance of happening on its own. Trying to orchestrate running into Stephen made me feel pathetic, and I was ashamed and embarrassed about how much time and thought I'd put into this, but none of that stopped me from doing it.

I would always recognize Stephen from several blocks away, both by the colour of his coat and the loping way he walked. As soon as I saw him, my stomach would contract with panicked excitement. And I would spend the next few minutes wondering if he would stop and talk to me today, or if he would just smile and say hi and keep walking. When he did stop to talk to me, I looked for extra meaning, either good or bad, in his words. Even if he didn't stop, seeing him was often highest point in my day.

I wondered if he ever thought about the party, or our aborted attempt to meet up for coffee. I wondered if he knew that I was angry at him, or that I had any feelings towards him at all. I mean, probably he knew – I'm not exactly the most subtle person when it comes to emotions – but it made me feel better to think that he was oblivious to the contents of my heart.

One day I somehow scraped together the courage to ask him out for coffee again. He seemed surprised that I'd brought it up again, but he didn't look like he was completely put off by the idea, so we set a time and place and I scampered off before he could change his mind.

I spent the next week dreading my meeting with Stephen. As before, I obsessed over every tiny detail – carefully planning what I would wear and say and do. I wanted to find the perfect combination of smart, funny, angry, forgiving, pretty, and nice-but-not-too-nice. I wanted to seem like someone who could call him on his shit, who couldn't be fucked with, but also, if I was being honest with myself, who he might want to get back together with.

If all this sounds impossible, that's probably because it was. We weren't going to get back together, we weren't even ever really going to be friends again, and I knew that. But I had to pretend that it could happen, because that was the last real hope that my heart was hanging onto.

So we met outside of the Student Union Building, as planned. I got there early, found a spot on a sunny bench and read my book; I kept reading even after I caught a glimpse of him out of the corner of my eye, because I didn't want to look too eager. And besides, I hoped that I might look pretty and thoughtful, sitting there with my nose buried in a book. Neither of us had any money for coffee, so instead we walked over to the lawn in front of the Arts and Administration building and sat there together. By then it was overcast, and the temperature was starting to drop, but still, we stayed and talked for over and hour.

At first we made general small-talk, about the program that he was in at school, and about his house and roommates. I wrote in my journal that he didn't seem to be as happy as he was making himself out to be, but maybe that was just wishful thinking. A lot of that conversation was wishful thinking on my part; even, or maybe especially, the assumption that Stephen actually wanted to be there, talking to me. I could tell that he was trying hard to grin and bear it, really making an effort to be sincere and polite, when all that he wanted for our talk to be over with. So after half an hour or so of indulging in my fantasy that we were just two friends hanging out, I cut to the chase.

It was pretty anticlimactic. I told him how I'd felt, both on the night of the party, and the day after, when I'd heard about what he'd say. He told me how he hadn't exactly minded my crying, but that he'd felt pretty irritated with me by the end of the night, when all he wanted was to go to sleep. He made it abundantly clear that I'd overstayed my welcome.

"And anyway," he said, "making fun of girls is just a thing we do in our house. It's not only you – we make fun of *everyone*. Or at least, everyone who's a girl."

He finished by apologizing, which didn't feel nearly as good as I'd thought it would. And then I tepidly suggested that we hang out sometime, to which he gave a totally noncommittal reply, something like, *Sure, fine, see you around.* I smiled and pretended that that was the response I'd been hoping for, then I lingered for a moment in case he was going to hug me. He didn't.

After that I went home and wrote up a list of reasons to kill myself.

It went like this:
Good Reasons To Kill Myself

1. No more money problems.

2. No more school problems
3. No more having to deal with Stephen and his idiocy
4. No more problems with friends, no more misunderstandings, no more fights
5. No more being frightened and nervous all the time
6. No more being sick, no more being tired, no more fear of my body
7. No more anything. Just a deep, blackness and insects crawling up my nose. Except that I plan on being cremated.

I then made a list of reasons not to kill myself:
Good Reasons Not To Kill Myself

1. Find out how the story ends.

What I meant by that was that I wanted to know how all of the loose threads would be tied up. I've always been a curious, maybe even nosy person, and the thought that my friends would continue living their lives without me – lives full of love and heartbreak, homes and jobs and friendships, raucous laughter and loud parties and grim mornings after and, oh, all of the other little things that make up our day to day existence – drove me crazy. I wanted to know where everyone would be in five, ten, even twenty years; I wanted to know if we would all be the same people, having the same problems, when we were bonafide grownups.

Of course, there was no better way to guarantee that I would be stay same person, *exactly* the same person, than to die young.

And I want to be perfectly clear here that I didn't want to kill myself because of Stephen. Oh sure, what he'd done and said had hurt, and the fact that he clearly didn't want to be around me also hurt. It hurt a whole lot. But on its own, that pain would have been bearable – it was just that I had to take it along with everything else, all the big and little shames and failures and embarrassments that had led to my present circumstances. On top of all of that stuff, it was just too much. Somehow, that conversation with Stephen was what finally convinced me that I didn't have a future.

Maybe it wasn't even the conversation itself, but how much it meant to me. The deep well of disappointment that I slid into afterwards was frightening, especially considering that I'd gotten everything that I'd purportedly wanted: a meeting with Stephen, an apology, a lukewarm offer of continued friendship. I should have been happy, or at the very least satisfied, but instead I felt worse than ever. And somehow, in the middle of all that hurt and sadness and fear, that sense of disappointment brought about one very clear, very rational question: *who was this girl?* This was not the girl who'd scored highest in the class on her first year final exam in Latin. This was not the girl who'd somehow managed to pull an A in Astronomy, which, while being a science class pretty specifically geared to arts students, was still a *physics credit*. This was not the girl who had fought to be able to go to university, who had moved three provinces away from home all by herself, who had thus far survived everything life had thrown at her. This was not *me*.

At that moment I realized that *that* girl, that smart, brave, resourceful girl, didn't exist anymore. I'd stopped being smart, brave and resourceful when I'd dropped out of school; because, really, wouldn't someone with all of those qualities have been able to figure out a way to finish her degree? And what *was* I, exactly, without that degree? Because I'd always planned my life out with the idea that I would do my undergrad in Classics, then go to graduate school, and then maybe teach. Then maybe I'd get married, live in a big house, have a couple of kids and write a book. But that future was gone now, and I hadn't found one to replace it. When I tried to think about what my life might be like in a year, or five years, all I could picture was an endless line of grey days, each with their own specific, yet similar, miseries.

At 21, I felt like like everything good was behind me, and my future was a cold, threatening blank.

Even my immediate future was frighteningly uncertain. It was only mid-October, but I already knew that I wouldn't have enough money for November's rent. I'd asked my parents for help, but neither of them could give me anything. Instead, my mother offered to pay for me to move back to Kingston. I tried to think about what that might be like; I pictured myself going home, a washed-up university dropout, and spending the rest of my days lonely and miserable while my family puttered on around me. I would have to watch my sisters grow older and smarter, accumulating piles and piles of successes while I lay on the couch and watched Star Trek marathons. Even worse, I would have to endure my family's pity, and then their inevitable why-don't-you-get-up-and-do-something, and then finally their acceptance that I was an absolute, total failure.

I couldn't go back to Kingston.

I also couldn't keep going the way I was in Halifax.

That week a couple of friends and I went to see a film called *The Event,* with Don McKellar, Sarah Polley, Parker Posey and Olympia Dukakis. It centered around Matt, a man in his thirties who was dying of AIDS. Instead of suffering the various indignities of the end stages of that disease, he decides to end things on his own terms. Because he wants to go out on a high note, he throws a huge party as a sort of goodbye and thank-you to all of his friends. Just as the party reaches its zenith, he retreats to his room and, with his family at his bedside, downs a cocktail of drugs that has been carefully selected for its deadly combination.

One of the main conflicts in the movie is the fact that Matt's mother is totally, steadfastly against his plan to commit suicide. She keeps trying to talk him out of it, right up until the very last minute. She just loves him so much, and wants to have him in her life for as long as possible.

But then, not long after Matt has passed out from his fistfuls of pills, he starts to vomit. And you, the audience, think, *Oh, no, he's going to wake up in the morning after all and have to go through all of this again.* But his mother reaches over and scoops the mostly-still-intact pills back into his mouth and holds her hand there, forcing him to swallow. She has this look of grim determination on her face, and you know that doing this is just about killing her. You know that his death is pretty fucking far down the list of things that she wants. But she's not doing this for her; she's doing it for him. And *oh*, that did a number on my heart.

Several scenes later, a few weeks after Matt's death, his mother calls his old number and listens to the greeting on his voicemail:

"Hi, this is Matt, I'm in heaven now. Leave your message and someone else will get back to you."

His mother pauses, then says,

"Hi Mattie, it's your mother. I know it's silly, but this is the only way I can still hear your voice."

She pauses again.

"I love you."

By the end of the movie, I was sobbing so hard that I couldn't talk. My friends walked me home in silence as I wiped my raw, red eyes and disgustingly snotty nose over and over on the sleeve of my coat. I kept thinking that I didn't want my mother to have to call my voicemail just to be able to hear my voice. But I didn't see any alternative.

It seemed like suicide was everywhere that month. A few days after I saw *The Event*, Elliott Smith died. From a self-inflicted stab-wound. To the chest.

And I thought, If this person, with his critically acclaimed albums and his dedicated fans and all of his fucking talent, can't manage to find a reason to live, then what fucking chance do I have?

After hearing the news, I lay on my floor and watched the suicide scene from *The Royal Tenenbaums*. I watched Richie Tenenbaum cut his hair and shave his beard, I watched him whisper *I'm going to kill myself tomorrow* to his reflection in the mirror and then I watched him slash his wrists, all to the soundtrack of Smith's Needle In The Hay.

I watched Richie come home from the hospital to find his adopted sister Margo lying in the Boy

Scout-style canvas tent he'd set up in his room. I watched her lean over an old plastic turntable and carefully place the needle on the waiting record; I heard the sound of The Rolling Stones' She Smiles Sweetly fill the cramped space of the tent. I watched him show her the stitches on his arms, watched them lie down on the child-sized sleeping bag and kiss. I listened to Margo ask if he was going to try to kill himself again, heard him tell her that he didn't think so. I watched her press her face into his shoulder and start to cry.

I sat through those scenes over and over, moving only to pause the video as soon as Margo said,

"I think we're just going to have to be secretly in love with each other and leave it at that, Richie."

After that line I would rewind it back to the part where Needle In The Hay started to play, and then watch the whole thing all over again.

I did this for at least an hour and a half, at which point my roommate came home and asked me what the hell was going on.

Hallowe'en was coming, and people were starting to piece together their costumes and trying to figure out which bars were throwing the best bashes. My friends half-heartedly asked me what I was going to dress up as, but I could tell that they didn't really expect me to go out with them. Who would want to take a sad-sack like me out for what was arguably the most fun night of the year? Kate, the only person who seemed to take a genuine interest in my Hallowe'en plans, kept trying to talk me into going to the party that she and her roommates were throwing. I knew that going to that party was a bad idea, and right up until I saw The Event I flat-out refused every time she asked me. After The Event, though, I started to change my mind.

I started to form a plan.

I would go to the party, I thought, and drink, and let loose. Stephen would certainly be there, since it was being held at his house, and I would prove to him and everyone else that what had happened at the last party was nothing more than a fluke. I would prove that I was a normal, happy person, a person who was funny and charming and talkative. I would flirt with all the boys there, simpering and smiling behind my drink. Stephen and his roommates would all realize how badly they'd misjudged me; maybe they'd even feel bad for the rotten things they'd said.

Then, afterwards, I would go home and shovel handfuls of sleeping pills into my mouth.

I would go out on a high note. I would go out with a bang.

As the day of the party approached, I wavered between the calm contentedness that comes with having finally made a difficult decision, and terror at the thought that I was making a horrible mistake. I knew that my relief and happiness meant that the decision to kill myself was the right one, but I couldn't stop myself from thinking *what if, what if, what if*. The calm certainty that I was doing the right thing managed to hold sway for a couple of days, but I found myself caught in a weakened what-if state during my next doctor's appointment. He asked me the same questions as always – Was I thinking of suicide? Had I made a plan? – and I fumblingly, hesitantly, told him about the upcoming party.

He put his pen down and looked at me, then turned and looked at the clock. It was late in the day by then, nearly five; I could tell he was disappointed that it wasn't earlier.

"I want you to go to the hospital first thing in the morning," he said. "I want you to see the psych nurse – she'll be in at nine. I'll call and tell her that you're coming. I want someone to see you right away. We can't sit and wait this out any longer."

Before I left, I watched him slowly and deliberately write SUICIDE RISK across the bottom of my chart. I felt strangely peaceful, as if I'd finally fallen as far as I could.

Was I in fact suicidal, though? I mean, really and truly? I've often asked myself that question in the ten years since that doctor's appointment, and I'm still not sure if I know the answer. On the one hand, if I'd actually wanted to kill myself, wouldn't I have just done it? Would a truly suicidal person really go to her doctor and, in essence, get him to prevent her from harming herself?

On the other hand, depression is a tricky beast; it thrives in grey areas, and its stock-in-trade is trembling uncertainty. Your sadness and self-loathing make you question yourself and your motives a thousand times a day. The only thing that you know for sure is that you are a terrible and stupid person, and who would ever trust a decision made by someone like that?

Maybe the best way to look at it is that it's like there were two of me. There was Suicidal Anne, who was exhausted and worn down after years and years of grinding sadness, but there were also vestiges left of Original Anne, the one who had existed before this whole mess had begun. Suicidal Anne was taking charge more and more often, to the point where she was almost exclusively the one running the show, with Original Anne mostly filling the role of concerned observer, able to watch but not intervene.

Somehow, though, Original Anne managed to wrench control for just long enough to rat Suicidal Anne out to my doctor.

I lay in bed that night and listened to my upstairs neighbours out on their deck. They were up until two or three o'clock in the morning drinking and talking, and although I couldn't make out what they were saying, the sleepy drone of their voices and the clinking of beer bottles was somehow comforting. After they finally went to bed I pried the screen off my window and leaned out as far as I could, chain-smoking and reading by the light of the streetlamp until the sun came up. I'd started smoking, I mean *really* smoking instead of bumming the occasional cigarette at a party, earlier that fall. My grandfather had recently died of lung cancer, a fact that had, up until then, prevented me from taking it up as a daily habit. Ever since I'd decided to kill myself, though, I'd been buying packs regularly. I mean, why not? I wasn't going to live long enough to get lung cancer, and I found the act of smoking to be very soothing – it gave me something to do with my hands, a sense of purpose or action which was otherwise lacking from my life.

At around eight o'clock, I got up, got dressed and ate breakfast. I packed the following items in my bag: my wallet, my discman, my book and my journal. As I set out to walk the short distance from my house to the Halifax Infirmary, I tried to figure out what I was feeling. Anxious? Definitely. Frightened? Maybe. Suicidal? Yes, still. Hopeful? Maybe a little. Hopeless? That too.

I walked through the hospital doors and into the emergency room, which smelled like fear, misery and rubbing alcohol. The seating area was all done up in 1970s palette of muted brown and orange, and there was the standard hospital-waiting-room issue television showing the local news mounted to the wall. This was the year that SARS had scared half the population of Toronto into wearing those dorky paper masks, and there were posters about it, accompanied by bottles of hand sanitizer, everywhere. I went over to the little triage room and sat reading a pamphlet about vaccination until it was my turn to go in.

There were two nurses working triage, and they took my temperature, blood pressure, and asked me all kinds of questions. I don't remember what, exactly, I told them, but I remember that they were kind – sympathetic, even. They told me that they'd a lot of people my age who felt the same way I did and that what I was going through was by no means rare. They told me that I'd done the right thing by coming to the hospital, and they hoped that I was feeling better soon. Somehow they knew exactly what I needed to hear, and a tiny flush of optimism spread through my chest. Maybe everything *would* be all right after all.

After scribbling a few notes on a clipboard and giving me sweetly encouraging smiles, the two nurses sent me around the corner to Emergency Room B.

I had to wait for nearly an hour before talking to yet another nurse in Emergency Room B, and she also took my temperature and blood pressure and went through the same list of questions that I'd already answered during triage. I asked if the answers I'd given an hour ago, not to mention my temperature and blood pressure, weren't already noted on my chart. The nurse just rolled her eyes and said that this was standard procedure. Then I sat for another two hours before I saw the psychiatric nurse.

The psychiatric nurse brought a medical student with her, and the two of them talked to me for about half an hour. She was very brisk – condescending, even – and very much in the pull-yourself-up-by-your-own-bootstraps camp. She kept asking me *why* I hadn't done anything to improve my financial situation – why didn't I have a job? Why wasn't I on welfare? Why had I let things get this bad before seeking help? I could tell that in her mind all of my current problems could be pinned squarely on my lazy unwillingness to shake this whole *depression* thing off and just get my shit together. Even worse, she asked me all kinds of probing, embarrassing questions about my life and my habits, to the point where she managed to make me feel even worse about myself than I had before setting foot in that damn hospital.

I cried during the entire interview, somehow managing to make my way through a box and a half of kleenex. Afterwards, they sent me away again, this time to wait for the psychiatrist.

I spoke to the psychiatrist, Doctor MacDougall, for all of ten minutes. He seemed preoccupied with something, and barely looked at me. He asked a few questions without seeming overly interested in my answers, halfheartedly jotted a few things down on a yellow legal pad, and then left abruptly. I was told that the doctors and nurses would have to confer and compare notes and sent back out into the hallway.

I settled into one of the hard, orange plastic chairs, and soon a boy about my age came and sat next to me. We studiously ignored each other, me with my face stuck in my book, and he with his eyes glued to the television. We sat there in silence for a few minutes before an orderly or maybe a nurse came over and told the boy that his admittance papers were ready to be signed. Except there had been some sort of oversight and no one had had the chance to sit down and explain to him what was happening. He started getting really worked up, yelling that no he fucking well was *not* being admitted, he was going home, and they needed to get on the phone right *now* and call him a fucking cab. Instead they called security, and while they were waiting for security to arrive they told him that they were going to admit him whether he signed the papers or not, so he might as well make it easy on himself and just sign the damn things already.

I thought, thank God that's not going to be me.

Two security guards came and escorted the boy away; he'd stopped yelling by then, and he didn't put up any resistance, but as he walked towards the door he kept muttering angrily to himself. I tried not to think about what would happen to him.

Not long after that, the doctor, nurse and medical student came and asked me step back into the little interview room.

They wanted to admit me, they said. If I didn't agree, they would have me admitted against my will, but it would be better if I cooperated. I needed help right away, they told me, and this was my only option. I asked if I could get treatment on an outpatient basis instead, but they said that the state of Nova Scotia's mental health care system was such that I would have to wait months and months for that. I balked, saying that I didn't feel comfortable doing any kind of inpatient program. I asked on what grounds they could admit me if I refused to sign the forms. They changed tactics then, implying that if I didn't want to be admitted, then I couldn't be so very depressed after all. If that was the case, then they wouldn't refer me to any of the outpatient services, because clearly I didn't need them.

I started crying in that desperate, panicked way that little kids cry. I cried so hard that I couldn't talk, couldn't even catch my breath. The nurse silently passed me a pen and the three of them sat across from me and watched me.

I signed, of course. What choice did I have? I was conscious of the fact that I'd been bullied into admitting myself, but I didn't know how to fight that bullying. What could I do in the face of the three people who held all of the power in that little room while I had absolutely none?

As I signed the small stack of forms, I asked if I would be able to leave if and when I wanted to. The nurse, all smiles now that she'd gotten her way, said that yes, because I was admitting myself voluntarily, I was free to go at any time.

Almost as soon as I passed the papers back to the nurse, a hospital commissionaire came to escort me to the psychiatric short stay unit. It was a long walk, to a separate part of the hospital called the Abbie J. Lane building. The name seemed like a funny combination of Abbey Road and Penny Lane and I suddenly wished that I had someone other than the commissionaire to tell this to. No one knew where I was, though – not my friends, not my roommate, not even the mother of the boy I babysat. Oh, I'd called her to tell her that I wouldn't be able to work that day, of course, but I'd given the flu as an excuse. My voice, rough and shaky from hours of crying, was enough to back me up, and she'd accepted my lie without question.

Once we reached the short stay unit, the commissionaire had to call to get someone to buzz me in. I heard the lock gently *snick* as the door closed behind me and the sound sent me into a full-on panic. I'd been crying ever since we left the emergency room, but now I started to sob even harder. The commissionaire, an older man with white hair and laugh lines around his eyes, just patted my hand and told me that I would be fine. Then he turned around and the door closed behind him and he was gone, slowly ambling back into the world of people who weren't locked in psychiatric wards. I turned around and found a nurse standing behind me; I told her, gasping and more than a little inarticulate, that I wanted to leave. I told her that the emergency room nurse had said that I could leave whenever I wanted, and I damn well wanted to leave this second.

She said that I couldn't leave, though, not until I'd spoken to the psychiatrist on call. So I told her to call the psychiatrist. She just sighed and rolled her eyes.

The nurse went into a glass-walled room and sat behind a desk; I watched her pick up the phone and mutter something into it; I could tell that she was muttering by the way she pressed her mouth to the receiver and barely moved her lips. She paused for a moment, nodding in agreement with whatever the psychiatrist was saying, then muttered something else. She hung up the phone, came over to where I was waiting and, a fake smile plastered on her face, suggested that I let her show me around while we waited for the psychiatrist to come.

The glass-walled room was, she explained, the nurse's station, where I could always find the nurse on duty. There was also a small closed-in room with a long wooden table where the staff held meetings and took breaks. After that, she showed me around the rest of the ward; most of it was a big, open space sort of set up like an open-concept house. There was formica-topped, institutional-looking table in the middle of the room, surrounded by half a dozen aluminum-and-vinyl chairs. In one corner there two ratty old couches and an ancient television, and in the opposite corner there was a dingy white-tiled bathroom, complete with bathtub and shower. All along one wall were our "rooms", which were really just small alcoves containing a hospital bed and a bedside table. These so-called rooms didn't even have doors on them, just heavy hospital curtains that could be drawn if the patient wanted privacy. Each room came equipped toothbrush, toothpaste, and a child-size paper cup full of viscous blue liquid that was both shampoo and body wash.

"You can leave your coat and bag here," the nurse said brusquely.

There didn't seem to be much point to that since I would be leaving as soon as I met with the psychiatrist, but I did it just to humour her.

After that I tried to call Denise, figuring that at least *someone* should know where I was, but she'd already left the office for the day. So I sat and read my book until the nurse announced that it was time to eat and ushered all of us patients towards the formica table. Supper was some sort of grisly meat in a pool of gravy with a side of instant mashed potatoes and green beans from a can, but I tucked into it eagerly. My financial situation had by then deteriorated to the point where I was eating No Name brand macaroni and cheese every night, so I was pathetically excited to find meat and vegetables on my plate. I only had the chance to eat a bite or two, though, before the nurse came over and told me that the psychiatrist was ready to see me.

They took me into the little meeting room where the psychiatrist waiting to talk to me. She had brittle, curly blond hair and spoke in a cold, clipped Eastern European accent. Without any preamble, she asked me why I felt that leaving the hospital was a good idea, and began taking copious amounts of notes as soon as I started talking. Meanwhile, I was struggling to pull myself together enough to properly explain why I wanted to go home. I began by telling her I didn't feel safe or comfortable spending the night there, and she nodded without looking up, indicating that I should keep going. Having already made what I thought was my strongest and most obvious point,

I thought fast to think of something else – unfortunately, the best that I could come up with was that I had a lot of laundry to do and it was my turn to wash the dishes and also I'd promised to call my mother that night. The doctor looked up then, frowning in a way that I knew meant that she didn't think I was very bright, and said that none of those were good reasons for leaving the hospital. I realized, then, that I should have just kept elaborating on my first point, rather than trying to come up with more.

Still, I said, they'd told me that since I was signing myself in voluntarily, I could leave whenever I wanted. And I wanted to leave.

The psychiatrist ignored that, and told me that if I wanted to call my mother, I could call her from the hospital.

No, I said quickly – too quickly – that was fine. I could call her the next day. It wasn't urgent.

But, the psychiatrist said, sensing that she'd found a sore spot, I'd listed that as one of the reasons why I wanted to go home. Didn't that mean that it was important?

The thing was, I explained, hesitantly, the thing was that my mother didn't exactly know that I was in the hospital. And I didn't want to tell her, because I thought that it would just worry her needlessly.

The psychiatrist smiled like a cat with a fat, wriggling little mouse pinned under its paw.

That settled it, she told me. If I'd agreed to call my mother, she might have let me go home, but since I hadn't, she wouldn't.

Unable to keep the note of triumph out of her voice, the psychiatrist went on to explain that this type of behaviour was known as *fragmentation*. Fragmentation is the fancy, technical term for only telling one or two pieces of the story to each person, but you never explain the whole of what's happening to any one individual.

It was a sign, the psychiatrist said, of a deeply disordered personality.

The worst of it was that she was right: I definitely did have a tendency to share only parts of the story and never the whole. At the time, when the psychiatrist first said this to me, I felt panicked, disoriented. Fragmenting, or whatever you wanted to call it, was something that I'd consciously done as a means of protecting myself and the people around me from my sickness; I'd never imagined that I might be making myself sicker. It was as if I'd been climbing and climbing a long flight of stairs, hoping that I'd find the exit soon, and then suddenly realizing that I was instead taking myself deeper and deeper into the labyrinth. And maybe there was no exit. And maybe all paths lead only to the heart of the maze.

Here I'd thought that doling out my life in bits and pieces was a smart self-preservation technique, a way of taking everything on myself so that I would never have to lean too hard on any one person or another. I had this idea that I would somehow figure out what information my various friends and family could handle, and then I could divide up my confessions accordingly. My reasoning went something along the lines of, *If I don't ever tell anyone anything that bores or upsets them, then it'll be easier for them to love me.*

The fact that I was difficult and frustrating to love was, I assumed, just a given.

These days, I'm less convinced of my unworthiness of love, and that fact alone almost certainly means that I'm much more mentally healthy than I was ten years ago. I try much harder to be honest about the parts of myself that I find shameful or embarrassing, and although that kind of vulnerability has been tough, it's a gamble that has more or less paid off. Having stripped myself down, often publicly, and having bared some of my darker aspects, I feel much stronger and happier. I'm glad that I don't compartmentalize my life to the extent that I used to.

That being said, I still don't entirely agree with the idea that "fragmentation" is the sign of a personality disorder. I may no longer convinced that it's the smartest, healthiest thing to do, but I also feel that it's a perfectly natural coping mechanism. When you get to a point where you just hate yourself so goddamn much, it makes total sense to think that other people would, if they knew the whole truth about you, feel the same revulsion that you do. It makes sense to want to hide what you think are the terrible, deal-breaker parts of yourself. It makes a whole fucking lot of sad, desperate sense. And, I mean, sure, in an ideal world everyone should have someone, or even better, multiple someone's, with whom they feel comfortable sharing all of themselves. In an ideal world no one would ever feel shame or guilt for things that they can't help, things like sadness or fear or loneliness. In an ideal world we wouldn't have so much trouble loving ourselves.

But we don't live in an ideal world, do we?

After the psychiatrist accused me of fragmentation, I began frantically scrambling to explain that no, it wasn't like that, really. I tried to tell her that everything that I'd said had come out exactly wrong. I wasn't whatever she thought I was.

It was too late, though. Ignoring my babbling, she stood up, walked across the room and pulled a piece of paper out of a filing cabinet.

"I didn't want to do this, but you leave me no choice," she said.

Of course, her tone and facial expression indicated that she didn't really give a shit one way or another over whether she did this, whatever *this* was, or not.

"What are you doing?" I asked, my voice cracking with fear.

"I'm certifying you."

"What does that mean?"

I felt like I might throw up.

"It means that I'm signing this so that you can no longer leave of your own free will," she said very calmly.

"No," I yelled, losing what few shreds of dignity I might have had left. "No, you *can't.* You can't sign that. They *told* me that I was here voluntarily. I'm allowed to leave. They said that. The nurse and the doctor, they *told* me that. You don't understand. This is *my life* you're fucking with. You can't just *do* this."

But it was too late, she'd already made up her mind.

For maybe the first time ever, I realized that, as so many other people have already said, free will is an illusion. Or rather, I realized that you only get to have free will if you agree to tow the line, do what you're told, and behave in the very specific way dictated by some fairly strict social codes. If you do all of those things, then sure, you might get a bit of leeway to do what you want. You might get a taste of freedom.

But that isn't really free will after all, is it?

This is how you end up in this system, I thought. You make one small mistake like saying that you don't want to call your mother. And maybe you have some very valid reasons for not wanting to call her, like maybe she's thousands of miles away, and you don't want to worry her over your current status as a psychiatric patient, a fact that she can do absolutely nothing about. Maybe you don't want to worry her because she's a single mother with two small children at home, and she already has way more than enough going on in her life without having to deal with a third kid who is suicidal. Maybe you feel as if you've spent your whole life trying not to worry your mother, and now it turns out that that concern is exactly enough to get you committed to the psych ward.

And now that you're in here, how will you ever get out? How do you fight against people who hear only what they want to hear, who manipulate your words so that they sound so much worse than they are, and who think that they know everything about you after only a ten minute conversation?

I saw myself spending weeks, maybe even months or years in the hospital, with no hope of ever being released. How would I ever get out when the doctors and nurses, who held complete control over every aspect of my life, weren't really interested in hearing a single thing that I had to say?

The psychiatrist indicated that our discussion was over, and one of the nurses led me back out into the main part of the ward and told me to finish my dinner. I couldn't, though; I was crying too hard, gasping my way through huge, panicked sobs. I ran over to one of the couches and collapsed there, choking on my tears and snot until I thought I might be sick. One of the other patients came over and tried to comfort me, but the nurse told her to leave me alone.

Then the nurse muttered something to herself about histrionics and went over to make a note on my chart.

At that point some small, mysteriously rational part of me realized that if I ever wanted to have any hope of being released, I had to calm down and do some damage control. Pretending to ignore the nurse's baleful stare, I went into the bathroom and huddled on the toilet, breathing deeply until I stopped crying. I splashed some water on my face, gave my reflection a fake, watery smile and then went back out into the ward. I walked over to the nurse and, as cheerfully as I could manage, told her that I wanted to make a phone call.

Instead of calling my mother, though, I called my roommate. I told him that I was staying over at Kate's for the night. Then I tried to call Kate, but she wasn't home; her roommate asked if I wanted to leave a message, but I just said no, I would try again later. I went back to the nurse and told her that I was done using the phone. When she asked if she could take my temperature and blood pressure, I smiled and said sure like a very normal, not-crazy person.

The nurse was silent while waiting for the thermometer to beep. She was silent while the black cuff puffed outwards, squeezing my upper arm and all the blood vessels it contained. The nurse kept up her silence as the mechanism clicked its released, the cuff slowly deflated and the dial on the machine told her something or other about my incomprehensible heart.

"Your temperature and blood pressure are both raised," she said eventually, her irritation evident. "But what else would you expect after all that crying?"

I told her that the crying had nothing to do with it. I told her that we both knew that the stress of being hospitalized against my will was making me sick. She just stared at me long and hard before finally telling me that I'd better smarten up.

I decided that the best way to smarten up was to start playing by their rules. I thought that if they saw that I wasn't fighting them anymore, if they saw that I was truly ready to be whatever it was they wanted me to be, then they would let me go. Wasn't that how it worked in movies? Or did that only work if you were being sincere?

Either way, I knew that I had to resign myself to staying in the hospital for at least one night; the psychiatrist had made up her mind, and nothing that I said or did was going to change it. I figured that instead of crying and carrying on, it would be best to use that night to prove to the staff that

I was a very happy, healthy, well-behaved person who definitely had no place in a psychiatric ward.

To that end, I decided to start befriending my fellow patients, because nothing says sane like the ability to nod, smile and empathize.

There were five beds in the short stay unit, and all of them were full that night, meaning that I had four roommates. The most gregarious of the bunch was a King's College student named Eddie. He must have been about my age, and he was there because he'd been found drunk and naked in the middle of the street, trying to get himself hit by a car. He'd done this, he explained, because his girlfriend had left him for another guy and his grandmother had died and something inside him had just snapped. He'd already been there for seventy-two hours at that point, and felt that made him something of an authority on the place. He was friendly enough, but very patronizing towards all of the other patients.

Next was Zsofia, an international student from Hungary. Zsofia had spent most of her childhood in Algeria, where her father had been a professor. They'd always been very close; he'd always taken the time to read to her, to share ideas with and explain philosophical concepts to her. Zsofia's father had always been her sense of home as they travelled around for his work. She'd been hospitalized after his recent and sudden death from a massive heart attack. Although she didn't blame herself, she did believe that her decision to study abroad had been selfish because it had meant missing out on the last few months of her father's life. She felt certain that she could never forgive herself for not being with him when he'd died, even though she admitted that no one could have had any way of knowing what was coming. She was very sweet and kind, easy to talk to and quick to cry. During my stay in the hospital, she sort of took me under her motherly wing.

The patient occupying the third bed was a girl named Emma Lou. A skinny blond loudmouth from somewhere out in the sticks, she was the type of girl to offer her thoughts and opinions long before they were ever asked for. She came from a family of drug-dealers, she said, and her life at home was driving her crazy. She told us that her sister had made the two hour drive from where they lived just to bring her to the hospital, and she'd had to beg and plead with the Infirmary staff to admit her as a patient, but now she couldn't wait to get out of this place. The short stay unit was bullshit, she said loudly, pointedly glancing over her shoulder at the nurses' station. It was, she said, fairly obvious that no one here was going to get the help they needed. She took smoke breaks every ten minutes like clockwork, swore like a stevedore, and had a deeply antagonistic relationship with the staff. She was discharged shortly after I arrived.

The fourth and final patient was a woman named Hannah who was nearly catatonic from all the medication in her system. She spent the entire evening on the couch, watching whatever anyone else put on the television. Even if someone turned the television off, Hannah stayed in her seat, her eyes glued to the blank screen. She must have been about eighty years old, and had been in and out of psychiatric hospitals since her early twenties. The only times she took herself out of her stupor were when she would suddenly and without apparent cause begin rambling about the shock treatments the doctors had given her back in the 1950 and 60s. The nurses were constantly coming over to ask if she needed to change her Depends.

I should have been able to muster up some kind of sympathy or empathy for Hannah, but I couldn't. All that I could think whenever I looked at her was, *That's going to be me in sixty years. I'll be alone in a mental hospital, shitting my pants and watching terrible television.*

I spent the rest of the evening reading alone on one of the shabby old couches, both of which were the colour of old vomit and smelled like institutional mildew and cigarette smoke. Later, around ten, I tried calling Kate again and finally got through. I told her where I was, and she breathlessly asked if there was anything that she could bring me. She was the type of person who thrived on this type of drama, and I could tell that she was rewriting the movie of her life to include a scene where she played the Helpful Friend to a Sad Crazy Girl.

"You know, your mom and your roommate called here looking for you," she said, unable to keep the excitement out of her voice. "I guess you haven't told them yet that you're in the hospital. They called before I got home and one of the guys here answered and now all my roommates talking about it. They all know that you lied about being here."

"Don't tell them anything," I said stiffly. "*Especially* not Stephen."

"Oh, I won't," she said, her voice oozing a believable sweetness and sincerity. "I promise."

I took a shower, then spent ten minutes combing out the greasy tangles left in my hair by the thick, lightning bolt-blue all-purpose cleaning gel. Since I didn't have any clothing other than what I was wearing, the nurse gave me a hospital gown to sleep in, and then another one to put on backwards as a sort of housecoat. I made myself some tea and toast, since I hadn't really had any dinner. They gave me a little paper cup full of sleeping pills, which I took without comment.

Just before I went to bed, another patient arrived to take over Emma Lou's bed. He was older, maybe in his sixties or seventies, and a rumour circulated that he was dying of liver cancer. He didn't, or maybe couldn't, talk to anyone; he just went and sat on his bed as soon as he arrived, letting the nurses open and unpack his bags for him.

Lights out was at midnight, and I lay in bed and read until the sleeping pills kicked in.

If I'd been someone who hadn't spent the last several months developing a high tolerance for sedatives, I might have slept through what happened next, but I wasn't, so I didn't. I woke to someone gently petting my arm, like you would a small, frightened cat. I jerked away, and looked over to see the new patient, the old liver disease man standing there. There was a night light out in the main part of the ward, and he was lit from behind, his face completely shadowed. His hand was still reaching out, as if he wanted to pet me again, and he was groaning quietly. My chest squeezing with panic, I scrambled out of bed and dragged the sheets with me, pulling them around me like a cloak.

"Get out of here," I hissed, terrified. "What are you even *doing* here? Get *out*."

At the sound of my voice, the man turned around and shuffled off into the corner of my little room. As soon as he was a few feet away from me, I bolted out into the ward trailing my blanket behind me, looking for someone, anyone, who could help. I ran as quietly as I could for the same reason that I'd whispered instead of yelling: I was worried about waking up the other patients. It was only after that I realized how funny it was to be so concerned about the quality of other people's sleep while at the same time feeling that I was in a dangerous situation.

There didn't seem to be any staff in the short stay unit, so I wound up following the labyrinth of hallways that lead to the main part of the psych ward. There, I found a single, solitary nurse sitting in the nursing station and reading a dog-eared romance novel. She looked up, irritated, as I came and stood in front of her.

"You're supposed to be in bed," she said. "Lights out is at twelve."

"There's a weird old man in my room. He was touching my arm. I'm over in the short stay unit, but there weren't any nurses there, so I had to come here."

At this point I was more angry than I was afraid. Why the fuck wasn't there anyone in my unit to make sure that we were safe? Didn't anyone know that it was a bad idea to leave five crazy people alone in a ward? What kind of place was this, anyway?

"He's probably harmless," she said, sounding bored. "Did you ask him to leave?"

"*Yes*, I asked him to leave. *Of course* I asked him to leave. He won't. You need to come get him out."

The nurse checked her watch, and then looked back up at me.

"I'll come by later. I can't really leave the desk right now. Sorry."

But she wasn't sorry. I could tell.

I walked slowly back to the short stay unit, thinking that I would camp out on the couch until the old man had left my room. I could use the sheet I'd wrapped around myself as a blanket, and when the nurses in our ward came back on duty and asked me why I was sleeping on the couch, boy would I ever give them an earful. Then maybe when I got out I would write a brilliant exposé about the mental health care at the Halifax Infirmary and everyone would realize how wronged I had been. That would fix those damn nurses.

I was starting to get excited about this idea, but when I peeked into my little sleeping area, I found it empty. So I climbed reluctantly back into bed and lay there, staring out into the dim blue ward. I knew that I should sleep, but I couldn't. Who knew what else might happen the next time I slipped into unconsciousness?

At that moment, I would have given anything to be back at my shabby old Creighton Street apartment, lying on the couch and watching re-runs of M*A*S*H. I was really into M*A*S*H that year; I found it strangely comforting to watch this group of lonely, mismatched people trying to make the best out of a living hell. I sometimes daydreamed that I was there, in the middle of the

Korean War, and that Hawkeye could be my best friend and together we would spend our days sipping martinis and trading witty quips. I could take lessons in assertiveness from Hot Lips and trade dresses with Klinger; maybe Colonel Potter would even let me ride his horse. I felt weird fantasizing about how great it would be to work at a war hospital, but the fact was that spite of all the gory, senseless death and destruction, everyone on M*A*S*H seemed to somehow be managing far better than I was in my comfortable, blood-and-guts-free life.

Lying on an army cot in a dank canvas tent that smelled of old sweat and mildew, waiting for the next round of wounded to come in so that I could devote myself to helping other people and maybe even saving their lives, seemed vastly preferable than being a being frightened and alone in a cold, clinical Halifax hospital bed.

This was at three o'clock. At six, I finally sat up and stopped pretending that sleep was a possibility. Instead, I pulled out my journal and began writing out an escape plan. The first thing that I would do would be to call Denise, I decided, and see what she could do; maybe she could even come and explain to the hospital staff that I didn't belong there. If that didn't pan out, then I would grit my teeth and call my mother; she was a social worker, after all, and I figured that she would know how to navigate this system better than I did. If neither of those things worked – well, I would just have to cross that bridge if and when I came to it.

I couldn't call Denise until her office opened at 9:00, so while I waited I sat down and had breakfast with my fellow patients. They ate all of their meals together, seated at a long table like students in a high school cafeteria or members of the same large, particularly cranky and tearful family. The only person missing from breakfast was Eddie, who must have been on a higher dose of sleeping pills than the rest of us. Instead of eating with us, Eddie lay in his bed snoring loudly for the entirety of the meal.

I called Denise and she said she would come when she had a break in her schedule, around noon.

"Do you promise to get me out of here?" I asked, my voice desperate.

"Anne, I can't promise anything like that," she said gently.

"But I'm not crazy! You know that I'm not crazy!"

"No one is saying that you're crazy, but you *do* need help."

"They think I'm crazy here!"

I caught the nurse looking at me, so I lowered my voice to a whisper.

"They think that there's something wrong with my *personality*. They think it's fractured or fragmented or something. I don't have a personality disorder, do I?"

"I don't think so," Denise said slowly. "I think you're very depressed. And I think you need help. What I'm not sure of is whether the hospital is the right place for you to get that help. I'll be there soon, Anne."

"They pressured me into signing myself in here, and now they won't let me go. I'm scared that I'll never be able to leave!"

"We'll figure something out, I promise."

To pass the time until Denise came, I hung out in Zsofia's room and let her do my makeup. She told me about her father, what he'd been liked, how much she'd loved him. We talked about death – because what else are you going to talk about in a ward full of suicide cases? – and whether or not there was an afterlife. She gently brushed all of the tangles out of my hair and tied it back into a neat braid; her hands were so lovely, with long, fragile-looking fingers that contained surprising strength. She sat back to admire her work and told me that purple eyeshadow brought out the colour of my eyes. She let me wear her perfume.

Later, Eddie came by and said,

"I heard you were on the phone."

I gave him the old side-eye, wondering where this conversation was leading.

"Yeah, I was. My therapist is coming today to get me out of here."

He just laughed and shook his head.

"Good luck with that. You're not gonna be discharged for at least a couple of days, maybe even a week. You're pretty messed up, I can tell."

"Yeah?" I said. "Yeah? I wasn't the one out running around drunk and naked trying to get myself *killed.*"

"I was in a crisis," he said smoothly. "That's not how I normally behave. I just had a bunch of fucked up shit happen in my life all at the same time, and I was having a hard time dealing with it. I'm not saying that what I did was smart, but it's not who I am. My life was fucked up, but it's gonna get better. But you? *You're* what's fucked up. And I don't think that's gonna change."

"Oh, fuck *you,*" I said to his back as he sauntered away, hands in his pockets.

While waiting for Denise, I discovered that there wasn't much to actually *do* in the short stay unit. Aside from a daily thirty minute meeting with "the team," an intimidating group made up of the staff psychiatrist, a social worker, a nurse, and a med student, the expectation seemed to be that the patients would just sit around wiling the time away. There weren't any books or magazines or board games lying around – I couldn't even find a deck of cards to play a round of solitaire with. The only entertainment came in the form of the flickering old television set. Since I've never been the type of person who's good at doing nothing,

I spent the morning alternating between chatting with Zsofia, reading my book, and pacing around the ward.

Finally, a nurse looked up at me from her seat behind the desk and said,

"Would you cut that out? You're making me nervous."

So instead of pacing I retreated to one of the couches and started writing in my journal.

I was scheduled to meet with "the team" around noon, and fortunately for me Denise showed up just as the meeting was about to get underway.

I'd never been Denise's biggest fan. She'd been my therapist for nearly six months at that point, and up until then I'd found her to be boring, patronizing, and generally a bit stupid. People always tell you that you need to shop around until you find the right therapist, but I didn't know, exactly, how therapy was supposed to make me feel, or what a good therapist would be like, so I stuck it out with old Denise. She was kind to me, and nonjudgmental, and those two things meant so much to me back in those days that I was willing to overlook a lot in order to get them.

Regardless of what I'd thought of Denise before, once she walked through the door of the short stay unit she became my favourite person ever; there wasn't anyone else on earth that I would have been happier to see, not even Stephen. I hugged her, hard, and pulled her into my little room. I started crying, again, and told her, again, that I was terrified of being stuck in the hospital forever.

"I understand your concerns," she said gently. "Don't think that I don't. But what I want, what we all want, is for you to be safe."

"But I don't feel safe here," I whimpered. "This place is awful. Please, please tell them to let me out. I promise that I'll never, ever even think about suicide ever again if you get me out of here."

She just smiled and squeezed my hand. Even though I knew that she couldn't promise to get me out of the hospital, I felt that, at the very least, I finally had someone with some amount of power on my side.

The psychiatrist opened the meeting by reiterating everything that she'd said the night before, adding that she found me to be "emotionally immature" and that it was her belief that I had "character problems" which would, without adequate treatment, develop into a full-blown disorder.

Then it was my turn to talk, and, remaining remarkably calm, I spoke about how I didn't feel that I would benefit from remaining in the hospital. I said that I was ready and willing to do whatever it took to be discharged, and asked them what they needed from me in order to achieve this. I repeated what I'd said to Denise, that I would swear not to commit suicide if only they would let me leave. I didn't end up mentioning the old man touching me in the middle of the night – to this day I've never told anyone that story, although I'm not sure why. Somehow it's always felt strangely shameful and embarrassing, as if what had happened had somehow been my fault.

After I finished, Denise began to speak and, God love her, she totally and completely backed me up on everything I'd said. She told them that she'd been seeing me as a client for six months and knew me well enough to believe that if I promised to not kill myself, then I would do whatever it took to make good on that promise. She said that she would act as a link between myself and "the team", and would make sure that I was hospitalized again if I started showing warning signs of suicidal behaviour.

Next was the social worker's turn, and she said that what she needed from me was a concrete plan for navigating the world outside of the hospital. Her biggest concern, she said, was that I seemed to have no solid plans for myself, and that allowed me to continually slide back into the same money-related traps that had been plaguing me ever since I moved away from home. And, of course, once I found myself in those familiar old traps, I started scrabbling to get out, my fingernails scratching uselessly at all the impenetrable walls that I had, according to her, allowed to be built around me.

It was when I couldn't find a way to escape that I really began thinking seriously about suicide.

And, I mean, I do understand the point that she was trying to make, but I think that what she failed to take into account was that I was someone who had, up until that fall, had a surfeit of plans. My plans had been to finish school, then go on to postgraduate work in my field until I had a PhD, complete with a complicated thesis focussing on some ridiculously minute detail of some ancient text. Or maybe I would dedicate my life to ancient languages, becoming so proficient in Latin and Greek that people from all over the world would come to me for new translations of old books. Or maybe I would become an archeologist like my aunt, and spend my days flying from one exotic locale to another, digging up treasures and perhaps, in the style of Indiana Jones, solving mysteries and having adventures.

The point that I'm trying to make here is that I'd *had plans,* and the world, for better or for worse, had conspired to take those plans away from me. Wasn't I allowed some sort of mourning period for those plans? Wasn't I allowed to grieve the life that I'd always thought would belong to me? Instead, I seemed to be expected to immediately come up with an entirely new direction for my life, one that apparently wouldn't involve higher education or money or anything like that. How could I possibly do that on the fly, when I'd spent years and years putting together the plan that I'd suddenly been forced to abandon?

I didn't say any of this in that meeting, of course. I could tell that they were getting ready to release me, so I just nodded my head and smiled a wan, watery smile, and agreed to apply for welfare and see a financial adviser. I also promised to continue seeing Denise until she felt that I no longer required counseling. After all of that, they finally agreed to discharge me after lunch.

I walked Denise to the door, thanking her over and over and over as we went. After she left, I had the great satisfaction of seeing the word *certified* removed from next to my name on the patient whiteboard.

After hungrily devouring a lunch of cold, congealed macaroni and cheese with canned peaches for dessert, I was free. Perfectly, beautifully free. I packed up my stuff, hugged Zsofia goodbye, and politely thanked the nurse on duty. The same commissionaire from the day before came back to escort me out; we smiled at each other in recognition when he came to get me. The sound of the door locking behind me was deeply satisfying; the sight of the empty, faux-granite-floored corridor in front was one of the most heartbreakingly lovely things I'd ever seen.

Outside it was raw and grey, just like pretty much any other autumn day in Halifax, but for once I didn't mind. I stood outside of the hospital taking in deep breaths of cold, damp, air that had the sharp, clean taste of saltwater. I felt euphoric; I don't think I've ever loved this dear, stupid old world quite as much as I did in that moment, and frankly, I'm not sure that I ever will again.

From where I stood, I could see Citadel Hill, and I spent a long time watching the cars circling the old stone fort that stood sentinel over the city. I watched a group of little kids playing soccer over on the Commons. I watched the big kids at Queen Elizabeth High School slouching against the red brick walls, trying to make it through a whole cigarette between classes.

I looked to the right, down the street to Camp Hill Cemetery and, past that, to the Public Gardens. I remembered how, when I was a kid, there was this funny green metal staircase in the Gardens that went up a few feet into their air before ending abruptly in a little fenced-in platform; it must have been some kind of lookout at some point, but whatever it was that you were supposed to be looking out over was long gone by the time I was born. We called it the Staircase to Nowhere and for some reason I'd loved it fiercely, always making a point of looking for it whenever we went to the Gardens and running up and down the stairs over and over, just because. When they'd torn the staircase down back in the late 90s, I'd been strangely, bitterly disappointed, as if it, and not the antique fountains or the cruel, lovely swans or the neatly manicured flowerbeds, had been the main attraction for me.

As I stood there, I thought about how I'd always pictured Nowhere as this place in the sky, way up in the clouds, where it was always shiny and bright and very still. A sort of secular heaven, I guess. I'd always thought that I'd end up in Nowhere when I died.

Now, though, it suddenly seemed much more likely that Nowhere was miserably cold, dark and numb. Nowhere was the cessation of all bad feelings, yes, but it was also the end of everything good. Nowhere was a deep, endless pit of nothing, and while that pit might have seemed attractive from a distance, standing at the lip of it gave you a much different perspective. Suddenly you realize that nothing means just exactly that: no thing, not one single thing, ever again. No familiar comforts, no objects for your hands to wrap around, no grey-green maritime sky flushing pink and orange with the sunset. Never the sound of your best friend's laugh as it slides into a raucous cackle. Never the scalding taste of fresh, milky, too-sweet coffee on a cold morning. No smells, not even the dead scent of earth and leaf mould and old rotting bones.

I thought about how if I died, I would never be able to slowly savour hot, buttery toast with a cup of loose-leaf darjeeling ever again. I would never read my heartaching way through J.D Salinger's

Franny & Zooey again. I would never lie on the kitchen floor while some hurricane pounded and smashed against my house. I would never see my troublesome family, never hear my mother say, "I love you Annie," never boss my sisters around again. It would just be nothing, all day, every day, except that there wouldn't even be days. It would be the absence of everything, forever.

In that moment, I knew that if I were dead, I would *miss* all of these things. And if I was able to miss things, that meant that I wanted them, maybe even liked them. And if I was still able to like things, then maybe I wasn't such a lost cause after all.

The truth was that all of those events and objects and feelings, even when taken together, did not make up an especially good list of reasons to live. But they were a start, weren't they? A place that I could jump off from, a place that I could come back to if I was ever unsure of how or where to go. A safety net.

And if I had a safety net, then maybe I'd never been in free fall after all.

I walked back to my house, slowly, savouring everything; although I'd only spent a little more than a day trapped in the dead, stale hospital ward, it seemed as if it had been much longer since I'd been in the world outside. Even just breathing the cold, damp air seemed like a remarkable act of freedom. I decided that as soon as I got home, I would call my mother and tell her that I'd been hospitalized, just to prove that psychiatrist and all her theories about my personality wrong. When I reached my building, I walked up the rickety wooden steps to my door, slid the key into the lock, and started to cry. I sat down on my stoop, pressed the heels of my hands against my eyes, and sobbed.

It had just hit me that I was finally back to being part of a world that allowed me to have control over as simple an act as whether or not a door was open or shut.

10.

There is no cure for depression. Not really. It's better – safer – to think of it as being, at best, a manageable condition. With the right treatment, the right combination of drugs and therapy and self-care, you can live a long, productive life. It's also helpful to think of it as the type of disease that comes in waves – months or even years of remission interspersed with periods of relapse. In a best case scenario, you might experience only one or two major depressive episodes in your lifetime, and then spend the rest of your time being a happy, valuable member of society. In a worst case scenario – well, in a worst case scenario the prognosis becomes much more grim. In a worst case scenario, depression can be fatal.

I've mostly been pretty lucky. I've had a few relapses since 2003 – mostly notably shortly after my son's birth in 2011, when I was hit hard with a case of postpartum depression – but I've managed to avoid being hospitalized again. That isn't to say that it's been easy, because it hasn't; just a few months ago I found myself in the emergency room of Toronto's Centre for Addiction and Mental Health, my mind hellbent on self-destruction. As much as I hate to admit it, when things get really bad my brain still short-circuits and starts whispering that dying is the only way out, dying is the only solution; and when that happens, it's so hard not to listen to my smart, usually credible brain. There were times – times, I should add, that have been few and far between – when I honestly didn't think that I would make it to my thirtieth birthday. But I did make it. I'm here. And I know that things could be so much worse than they are.

I still live in Sadness, and I probably always will. I try my best to stick to the borderlands and never stray too far from that other world, the world where almost all of the people I know and love still live. On a clear day I can see that world perfectly, and can interact with the people there as if there isn't an invisible line between us. On the good days I never stray from the familiar paths.

It's so easy, though, to step off the path. It's so easy to be drawn away from the edge of Sadness, deep into its dark, tangled heart. You might find yourself pulled there by forces you don't understand, or else you might believe that the journey is your own choice, as if you're a sort of explorer or adventurer set on bringing back something strange and exotic, an as-yet-unseen piece of Sadness to be dissected and categorized.

You might think that you can make it to the root of Sadness and back safely, but that's an illusion. All voyages inward are equally dangerous.

11.

The title of this book comes from a passage in J.D. Salinger's *Franny and Zooey;* it's part of an exchange between Bessie, the middle-aged matriarch of Salinger's beloved Glass family, and her twenty five year old son, Zooey. Bessie (who, it should be noted, has come into the bathroom uninvited to sit and smoke while Zooey takes a bath) makes an innocent remark about the title of a screenplay that her son is reading.

"'The Heart Is an Autumn Wanderer,' " she read, mused, aloud. "Unusual title."

The response from behind the shower curtain was a trifle delayed but delighted. "It's a what? It's a what kind of title?"

Mrs. Glass's guard was already up. She backed up and reseated herself, a lighted cigarette in her hand. "Unusual, I said. I didn't say it was beautiful or anything, so just-"

"Ahh, by George. You have to get up pretty early in the morning to get anything really classy past you, Bessie girl. You know what your heart is, Bessie? Would

you like to know what your heart is? Your heart, Bessie, is an autumn garage."

That line – *your heart, Bessie, is an autumn garage* – has stuck with me all these years, ever since I first came across the book in my late teens. Whenever I read it, I always picture my grandparents' garage in Nova Scotia, which was its own separate building a few dozen feet away from the house. I think of the boxes and boxes of books that my grandfather kept in there, boxes that took ages to sort through and catalogue after he died. I think of all the other stuff stored in the garage – his tools, baskets full of hardware, old furniture that he was refinishing to sell at his antique store. Most of all, though, I think of him. I think of him with his wavy grey hair and his thick grey beard, sitting on an creaky wooden chair by the garage door and holding forth on anything and everything. I think of how his eyes creased when he smiled, the rough calluses on his hands, the gruff sound of his voice.

We always left Nova Scotia at the end of the summer, just as the leaves were starting to turn and a damp autumn breeze blew in off the bay. The end of August is when the light begins to change; it's still strong and bright during the day, but becomes melancholy, even a little desolate in the waning afternoons and long, dreamy evenings. Late-summer light, from the days when the world teeters on the divide between the hot, green summer and the slow descent into the cold heart of winter, is what nostalgia is made from. Autumn is the season of endings, of barren fields and bonfires and celebrations for the dead. Autumn is the season of packing up, storing away, battening down. Autumn is always, still, the sweetest ache I've ever known.

My heart is an autumn garage. My heart is a rickety old building filled with memories and artefacts. My heart is a dim room lit by sad, grainy light filtering through dirty old windows. My heart is a storehouse of everything that was once useful in my life, some of which might, someday, be useful again. My heart is waiting for the coming winter, its shutters and door ready to swing shut at the first sign of snow. My heart can weather the blizzards, can last months buried in deep drifts of snow. My heart is brave. My heart is a survivor.

Most of all, though, my heart knows that autumn always, always carries with it the promise of spring.

ACKNOWLEDGMENTS

Enormous thanks and much love to the following people, without whom this little book would not have been possible:

Annie, Ryan, Audra and Chris, who took the time to read my earliest drafts and who offered invaluable criticism and much-needed cheerleading.

Nathan, who very wisely told me to be kinder to my younger self.

All of the people, too many to name here, who told me to keep going when I needed to keep going, and encouraged me to step back when it was time to step back.

My mother, Lorell, and my sisters, Catherine and Claire, who are always supportive and loving no matter what.

Theo, for just being Theo.

Matt, for carrying the extra load whenever I need room in my pack for that metaphorical oxygen tank.

ABOUT THE AUTHOR

Anne Thériault is a Toronto-based writer, agitator and general smarty-pants. Her blog, The Belle Jar – which was the name she would have given her all-girl punk band, had she ever started one – is a collection of essays on feminism, social justice, mental health, and parenting. She is very opinionated and loves cussing a lot.

Made in the USA
San Bernardino, CA
20 December 2015